Texas and Christmas

Within the stereo view card image:

Sold only by Griffith & Griffith

Philadelphia, Chicago, London, Hamburg, Ger., St. Petersburg, Russia

Geo. W. Griffith, Publisher

2048. Dear Old Santa Claus Has Something for All.

Stereo View Card—Collection of Darnelle Vanghel

TEXAS *and* CHRISTMAS

A collection of traditions, memories, and folklore

edited by Joyce Gibson Roach

TCU Press
Fort Worth, Texas

Library of Congress Cataloging-in-Publication Data

Texas & Christmas : a collection of traditions, memories, & folklore
/ edited by Joyce Gibson Roach.-- 2nd ed.
      p. cm.
  ISBN 0-87565-289-1 (trade pbk. : alk. paper)
  1. Christmas--Texas. 2. Texas--Social life and customs. I. Title:
Texas and Christmas. II. Roach, Joyce Gibson.
  GT4986.T4T49 2004
  394.2663'09764--dc22
                                        2004004956

Printed in Canada

Contents

Always to my mother, Ann,

who still keeps Christmas for four generations of us—

Darrell, Delight, Trey, and Hollyann.

Introduction

Throughout the world, Christmas is probably the most special day of the year. And everywhere, from Maine to California and beyond the ocean, it is different in each community, each home. Yet those of us who like to think Texas is special believe that Christmas here is bigger, better, and more treasured than anywhere else. This collection, first published in 1983, grew out of that conviction.

Most of these pieces bring the past into the present, reviving traditions and memories of Christmases long gone. Others reflect the diversity of our Texas people, and still others describe customs that are even today setting new traditions for the future. The many cultures of Texas are reflected in memoir, poetry, and recipes, and there are stories for the young, the old, and the young at heart.

Want to make syllabub? The recipe is here. Curious about the way African Americans in East Texas or the Germans in South Central Texas celebrated? Helen Green and Minetta Goyne capture those special customs. Elmer Kelton and Joyce Roach recall the joy and sadness of Christmases during World War II.

When it was first published in 1983, this small book enchanted readers young and old. Now it has been revised and expanded—new memories have been added, new activities suggested, new traditions explored.

Stereo View Card—Collection of Darnelle Vanghel

Freeze-Frame:

Christmas as I remember It

SOMETIMES it seems to me that when I was a child, Christmas lasted all winter. Because snow and ice are a rarity in the southerly parts of Texas, we had none of the distractions of winter sports. The holidays began the last week of November, about the same time as the coldest portion of the year. Some years Thanksgiving came first, some years the birthday of my great aunt whose house was across the street from ours.

Tante Marie was special in more ways than one. Of the living members of our family, only she had been born in Europe, and in a castle, no less! Only she of all the family had remained a practicing Catholic. The only spinster of her generation and never blessed with robust health, she received much solicitous attention from all her kin. Because it was Mama who never needed encouragement to orchestrate a social gathering, it was usually she who arranged for Tante Marie's birthday party. On that day most of the oldest ladies of the town would come to our house for what, had we been

English, would have been high tea. In our town, where many people spoke German or Spanish in preference to English, almost every German lady belonged to a "Kraenzchen," a group that celebrated their birthdays together. As the ranks of Tante Marie's contemporaries thinned, the empty places were filled at first by nieces, then by grandnieces, and finally, after the celebration had been moved to the nearest Sunday, by the men and boys of the family as well. Result: two family feasts in one week, and this when the Christmas season was barely a flip of the calendar away! A few days before Pearl Harbor, I made the short train trip from college to my home for the last of Tante Marie's birthday parties. The next summer she passed away in her ninety-third year.

The real Christmas season began when Mama would recruit any of us children willing to help gather cedar greens for wreaths. A trip to our grandmother's ranch just west of town always met with our approval, whether it was to gather mustang grapes or agaritas for preserving, to explore the cave, or just to be in the country. For days after we had collected the evergreens I would come home from school to find Mama sitting on her heels on the kitchen linoleum, forming wire coat hangers into cir-

cles, then wrapping the waxed green cord around innumerable tufts of fragrant cedar until at last there was a plump wreath, looking like a looped green foxtail, the hook of the hanger hidden by a bright red bow. One wreath was reserved for decorating our front doorway with its beautiful ovals of beveled glass. The rest were put into a huge cardboard carton, some to be delivered to special friends, others to be taken to the cemetery. Our deadline was the birthday of Tante Marie's father, the great-grandfather who had brought his family from Austria and whose memory was lovingly preserved through many a relic and story. It was unthinkable that his grave be left bare on December second.

Now the family graves are variously neglected or else covered with a carpet of manicured grass, a convenience to those who provide the so-called perpetual care for a fee. But the blend of fresh cedar, musty decaying flowers from the last visit, and dampened dust of the gravel that used to hover there still seems to cling to the flowers that assert their brilliance or sit in ghastly greyness bleaching in the Texas sun. The sense of loss that I take with me as I leave is deflected from the occupants of the graves to the alienating ambience of the place. I turn hopefully to the living.

The house where I grew up is rented now to strangers. As I drive by to make a cursory inspection of the property without even getting out of the car (on either side are parking lots for churchgoers now), I see an unlighted string of Christmas globes framing the front porch, though it is April. They were there the last time too, in October. A flip of a power switch has become the difference between a never-ending observance of Christmas and the darkness of all other nights. Has Christmas become more of an effort than it is worth? The lady of the house has a full-time job in town. At this hour all I hear, as my car creeps by, is a shrill bark from what was our parlor. Even before the street was paved, when a mule-drawn wagon sprinkled the crushed stone, Papa thought there was too much traffic to allow me to have a dog. The unswept front path seems waiting for me to perform my earliest chore. The giant pecan that the squirrel planted as Papa watched from the dining room is dying, one limb at a time. The low wall that never had a purpose beyond dignifying the approach to the front door is buckling where roots buttress the shrubs. I am grateful that diseases, storms, and the power company have respected the beauty of the old elm grown from a sapling that

3

Papa brought in on horseback long before I was born. My uncle used to tie his horse there after having it shod at the blacksmith's a block away from our house and directly across from the post office. The ringing of the anvil and of the church bells next door were my alarm clock when this was home.

One of my earliest memories is of waking up and groping for the drop-sides of the white iron crib that confined me in the huge, dark, unheated room where all our family except Papa usually slept. Of the wood-burning stoves upstairs, the one in this tremendous glassed-in porch was seldom used except when Mama needed the sewing machine or had invited ladies over for a quilting party. At this particularly memorable daybreak I could not see the ribbed cotton stocking at the foot of my bed, but I could feel that St. Nicholas had not neglected to fill it. It was probably in the manufacturer's hideous verison of flesh pink, because for this purpose Mama avoided using our black stockings since the lint might stick to the goodies and the white hose because the treats might discolor them. How I hated those stockings worn with garters just above the knees! But, folded over the railing and pinned to itself with a huge safety pin, this one stocking was now the sole object of my

desire. In its toe was what felt like a tangerine, a treat much preferable to an orange, being so much easier to peel and to nibble in the dark. There were also some English walnuts and a little toy: a whistle perhaps, a celluloid doll or animal, some small game or puzzle. A few years later this was how I would acquire my first yo-yo, with which I became far more proficient than I ever managed to be with my brother's string top. As the sky grew paler, I pulled my plunder under the eiderdown feather bed that had warmed one member of the family after another since Papa's grandmother had brought it with her from the Rhineland as a girl. That particular morning someone else in the room finally woke up and let down the side of my crib so that matters made more urgent by the chill of the room and by my excitement could at last be attended to.

When I entered school—the Catholic school behind our house—it struck me as odd that my churchgoing schoolmates seemed less well acquainted with my favorite saints than were all of our free-thinking family. For, having hung up our stockings on the eve of December fifth to receive Saint Nicholas, we hung them up again in exactly the same way about two weeks later, ostensibly to get a kind of progress report on our behavior from Saint Thomas. I have wondered whether our family gave him the label "lazy" instead of the more conventional "doubting" because of their own skepticism. Certainly to us laziness led to reproaches, whereas doubt was to be expected in matters of religion. My own blind faith consisted mainly of believing that "der faule Thomas" truly would bring a lump of coal to admonish youngsters who did not measure up, though I never actually knew a child who received such a rebuke. Instead, each of us was usually given on this occasion, in addition to a piece of fruit and some nuts, some candies of various sorts that most American children of my generation will recall: tiny, naked licorice dolls that, without a qualm, we called "nigger babies"; little barrel-shaped hard candies flavored and colored like root beer; paraffin bottles filled with cloying syrups; and pastel fondant molded to the shape of seasonal motifs and sparkling with coarse granulated sugar. Rather than a fragile candy cane, there might be a peppermint stick wrapped in wax paper, for cellophane and all its successor plastics came later, and foil was reserved for cigars and chewing gum.

After I entered school, part of the joy of the season was the weeks-long cluttering of the classroom with drawings and construction paper cutouts. I do not remember that there were advent wreaths with candles or even advent calendars, though these are German customs and many of our teachers were nuns from Germany. I cannot even remember seeing such in our stores then, though other imported goods were stocked regularly. Many of our nicest toys, though usually not big ones, and almost all our ornaments were made in Germany and were in some cases so fragile that one wondered how they had withstood the trip. Many lasted to delight more than one generation of children, actually. The tradition of the Christmas tree itself is attributed to the Germans, and when I discovered that our Austrian ancestors had emigrated from a place only a few miles distant from the village where "Silent Night" was composed, I imagined that Christmas as we observed it had authenticity like no other.

In the school we attended, the younger of my older sisters and I were among the few non-Catholics, but—because we lived right by the church, the school, the convent, and the priest's home—we were often the very children who helped the nuns prepare for church celebrations. Some of my nicest Saturdays were spent in polishing the censers, arranging flowers for the altars, or stamping out wafers the Reverend Father would then bless to use in the Holy Eucharist, a ceremony in which I could not participate. When Mama proposed some disagreeable chore at home, I was not above saying that I must not go back on my promise to the Sister Superior to help put the sacristy in order. If the autumn had been especially gentle, the lady next door, a staunch daughter of the church, would cut the poinsettias that grew roof-high on the south side of her house, seal the stems with a burning match, and give the enormous flowers to the sisters as decorations.

The flowers, the statuary, the manger scene, the incense, the chants: these were my introduction to drama. Here the men and boys sat on one side of the aisle, the women and girls on the other; at the only other theater I knew then, the division was horizontal: brown in the balcony, white downstairs. I have since often wondered whether our town's few blacks went to the picture show at all. I suppose that they were of the Santa Claus persuasion, but until I was almost ready to enter school, I knew hardly a child who spoke only English, hung up a stocking on Christmas Eve, or received gifts in the morning from that "jolly old elf." Our "Weihnachtsmann," a sober-looking gentleman, was always in an ankle-length robe that was as likely to be light blue as red, and his distinguishing equipment was a pilgrim's staff or the shepherd's crook of a bishop. An ascetic rather than a gourmand, he was known to me only from pictures or our German tree ornaments. To us he came only in spirit, and I never believed that the unadorned little evergreen he was always pictured as carrying had any connection with our Christmas tree.

Between the visits of "Nicolaus" and "der faule Thomas" there fell my own birthday, but little was made of that day, it being outranked by all the surrounding festivities. Statistically a year older but no better able to control my mounting tensions than before, I faced the temptation of coming home daily to the aroma of cookies baking. Once, in an attack of hubris that was much like the zeal that would seize her whenever she caught sight of a bountiful harvest worthy of preserving, Mama baked seventeen varieties of cookies, but when some of us could not be converted to accept the new sorts as favorites, she was forced to concede we were conservatives and had to content herself with the usual dozen recipes.

As much the youngest child of the family, I pretended not to grasp what was going on the afternoon of

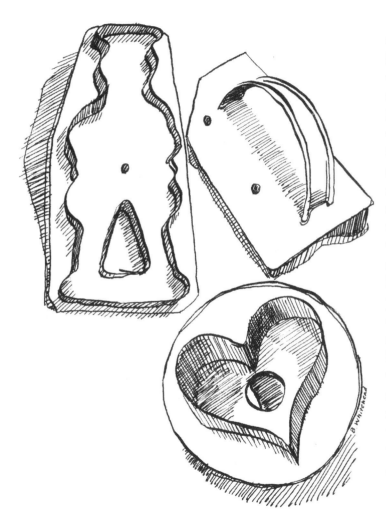

Christmas Eve, even long after I had in fact lost my innocence. My brother, in college before I was four, would climb the ladder into the attic to fetch the tree ornaments, then sneak them down the stairs to the parlor, where the tree had been moved from the pail of water that had been keeping it in the storeroom under the stairway, a place we called the "Rumpelkammer." All afternoon he and my sisters would trim the tree, occasionally popping out for a moment with much ado about not letting me see. Mama, meanwhile, would try to distract me by requiring armful after armful of stove wood that, when I was very little, she still used for cooking but later just for heating. My special treat was being allowed to help cut out the last of the cookies, picking my favorites from among the large number of cutters she kept in a box. Each year there were laments about how some rusty and brittle forms would have to be copied, or else—horror of horrors—discarded. If the weather was very warm, I might be sent out to play awhile, but only in parts of the yard from which I could not look into the parlor, which was very limiting, since there were no doors separating the three front rooms of the house, only archways. Once, I remember, there were shrieks when a shade suddenly flap-flap-flapped, as shades with springs are inclined to do. But I had not timed my entrance right. I thought I wanted to see inside, and yet, when once I did unintentionally glimpse the colored tree lights reflected in the glass of the front door as I came in at the back of the house with some wood, I felt profoundly guilty and said nothing about it. Preserving my illusions was too important to the rest of the family, as I dimly recognized.

My brother and the oldest of my sisters claimed to remember when Papa had still insisted the tree have candles. That Mama had kept a bucket of damp sand in the parlor in those days as a safety measure I could well believe, because both Mama and Papa had experienced destructive fires as young people when living in the country. Sure enough, when I got big enough to help with the tree, I found among the ornaments some tin candleholders equipped with clamps for attaching them to branches, and on some there was melted wax. Thereafter I was prepared to accept this like most other family stories, apocryphal or not.

On most workdays, including Saturdays, Papa would come home at sundown. On Christmas Eve it was mid-afternoon when he left the quarry he supervised. While he switched from his lime-covered clothes, I would change from coveralls and tennis shoes into a dress and black patents. Transformed, we two would go in the family car to call for his parents. Since these were among the few occasions I had Papa to myself, how is it possible that I have not a single memory of the conversations that must have taken place as we drove across town to where the old people had moved from the farm shortly after my birth? They were our only guests for Christmas Eve, we their only descendants who lived within hundreds of miles of them. After Grossmutter died when I was seven, Grossvater chose to break the Christmas Eve pattern. His one try at continuing it had evidently proved too depressing. I was too thoughtless then to wonder what he did instead, alone or with his housekeeper, and since he was an extremely reserved person, I never felt free to inquire of him later.

When Papa and I arrived at our destination, Grossmutter would pretend to be not quite ready, only for the purpose of increasing my suspense probably. She would invite me to sit on her bed while she took care of some maddeningly trivial matter such as adjusting her hair or selecting the right embroidered handkerchief. In the background we could usually hear Papa and Grossvater talking, perhaps arguing about Hoover and

Roosevelt, about whom they did not entirely agree, or listening to the Atwater Kent, for they had a radio at that house before we did at ours. Grossmutter preferred her records of John McCormack and Alma Gluck, but on this night of nights their tastes converged as they would listen to Madame Schumann-Heink sing the "Ave Maria," but whether the Bach-Gounod or the Schubert I cannot say, because I usually busied myself with thumbing through *Holland's* Magazine in the hope of finding a new Dolly Dimples paper doll. Besides, I did not know one version from the other in those days. There was always some mention of the fact that Madame Schumann-Heink had had sons on both sides during the war. Sad though this made me, I could not understand what this had to do with the adult's enthusiasm for the contralto voice, since I was never able to judge with certainty whether the deep tones emanated from a man or a woman, and a child likes to be sure about things like that.

Most of what transpired until we got back to our house made little impression on me in my excited state. I cannot remember our entering, the others greeting the grandparents, or much of anything else. In fact I can recall only a few of the gifts from those early Christmases: a kiddie car, and later a tricycle; Tinkertoys; almost always a book from a childless aunt in Indiana whose sister, a librarian, helped her make a selection; my first new roller skates, long after I had become skilled with the family hand-me-downs; some red leather house shoes with white lamb lining and cuffs that I liked so much I never let on they were already a bit too short. Somehow I knew Mama had bought them on sale, so they could not be returned anyway. One year there came a box of marzipan made to look like cold cuts, the gift of Papa's cousin, a schoolteacher in New York City. It was a novelty I accepted as warily as I did Madame Schumann-Heink's voice. Days passed before I would risk as much as a bite.

Sometime during the thirties we stopped having native cedar trees from my grandmother's ranch and started buying fir trees at the Mexican fruit and vegetable stand we patronized. Several relatives had come to believe that the cedar pollen caused the colds they always suffered as part of Christmas. I do not know whether their colds then stopped or not. Originally our tree was always mounted on the library table in the parlor, the trunk of the tree stuck into the hole of an enormous oxcart wheel, one with a solid center, not spokes.

I do not know the source of the wheel or its ultimate destiny, but the great round thing was covered with a drapery of velvet whose original dark green had faded interestingly into a variety of metallic hues ranging from copper to brass. In the folds there were always beards of grey Spanish moss into which had been nestled some polished red apples and large oranges. With the passing days the fruit would approach decay, growing more and more pungent. Only then were we encouraged to eat it.

When we changed from a cedar to a fir, Papa discovered that one must cut wedges to drive into the hole of the old wheel to prevent the tree from toppling, since the trunk of the fir was more slender than that of the cedar. After a year or two, one of Papa's workers made a new stand, totally without the charm of the old one, looking somewhat like an obelisk and enameled in a truly inappropriate shade of green. Now our trees might be more stable, but they were certainly not as impressive as before. For one thing, they had to be smaller; for another they were moved from the center of the room to a place by the front windows. This was particularly disconcerting to me, because this was the little freehold I had always used for displaying my gifts. We all left our gifts in the parlor for a week or more, until the traffic of guests started to thin after New Year's. Viewing gifts of others was part of the entertainment in those days, since ordinary people did not receive such things throughout the year then. This was not ostentation or conspicuous consumption, but just another part of the pleasure one shared.

Shortly before noon on Christmas Day the several units that constituted our extended family would gather at the home of Mama's mother on the ranch. Oma was the matriarch, beyond a shadow of a doubt, although the youngest member of the oldest generation attending. She was seventeen when my mother, her oldest child, was born. Since Mama was almost forty-one when I first saw the light of day, Oma was exactly my present age, it suddenly occurs to me. I was her youngest grandchild, the only one near the age of her grandson Franz, my cousin who was growing up in her house and the home of his father and stepmother a few yards away, his mother having died before he was two. As both houses were on top of the highest hill in the area, and Oma's had a tall square observation tower to boot, one could see for miles around. Especially beautiful was the sight of the lights coming on at sunset in the town in the valley below.

A visit to Oma's involved a trip of exactly the right length: long enough for a complete change of scene, yet short enough for me to sustain a good humor though wedged between adults and nearly grown children. The three miles from our house in the middle of town to Oma's house on the ranch prevented my being with my cousin Franz often enough for us to become bored with one another's company. The implications of his peculiar situation escaped me in those days. In fact, I considered him to be very fortunate to have not only two homes but also five doting grandparents, to four of whom he was at that stage the only grandchild. The one grandparent he had to share was Oma and, because he usually slept and ate at her house, she was at his beck and call most of the time too.

The final notes of the overture that preceded our entering Oma's house were always the same. For the last few hundred feet of the climb Papa would have to shift gears not once but twice, a maneuver that always retained a certain charm for me. The first thing we would do when we got out of the car was to check the trunk of the "bodark" tree by the garden gate to see whether the hitching ring Opa had inserted into the tree trunk was continuing to disappear at the same rate. My brother and the oldest of my sisters could remember when the iron ring could still be moved up and down freely; by the time I was big enough to notice it, the ring was hidden beyond its middle so that it seemed to be swallowed up at a faster and faster rate. By the time I was grown up the entire thing was almost scarred over with bark. I always wanted to gather the bright green "osage oranges" that lay scattered about, but was dissuaded because of the stains they left on one's hands.

I cannot remember Oma's Christmas trees well, but they were always huge, rotund cedar trees my uncle had cut in the pasture, and they sat directly on the floor, as I recall. It seems to me that they had an abundance of tinsel rope, something we scarcely used at our house at all. The ornaments were not particularly interesting, being newer and far more ordinary than ours. This house had been built on the foundation of the one that burned when my parents were first married, and few of the contents of the old house remained. At our house the old ornaments were from Papa's parents, acquired when the old people stopped having a tree of their own. Perhaps it was my cousin's electric train set that encircled the tree to which I should attribute my foggy recollection of Oma's Christmas trimmings, but she was of a very practical bent, having grown up on a western Texas ranch and not much inclined to take a great many things of that sort very seriously.

Present at Christmas dinner were usually, besides our household and the folks that lived on the hill, Mama's sister and her family, and—since they had no close relatives besides their grandchild, son of their only offspring—Franz's maternal grandparents, an eccentric old couple who always treated me very kindly because I was a special playmate of their sole reason for going on after the death of their daughter. Besides Tante Lina, Onkel Carl, and their two daughters, girls about the age of my older siblings, there were sometimes also the parents of Franz's stepmother and their two daughters, so that of the big children present my brother was the only male. In the course of the afternoon, as the time for coffee and cookies approached, we were sometimes joined by my other grandparents who, because they had a car, generally picked up Onkel Joe and Tante Mathilde, who lived near them. Onkel Joe was brother to both Opa and Grossmutter, my parents being cousins. If she had not chosen to go to the home of a brother or sister,

there would also be Onkel Joe and Tante Mathilde's unmarried daughter, who worked, as husbandless ladies of nice family then often did, at a local millinery, another institution that has gone the way of the buggy whip. Since Tante Marie had come with us, if she had not made other plans, that usually completed the group.

The menu varied little from year to year. Oma prepared the turkey and a sort of dressing, more like a meatloaf than a side dish, a combination of bread, eggs, parsley, and the indigenous kind of smoked sausage, all of the ingredients forced through a grinder before being stuffed into the turkey to bake. Papa was officially in charge of carving, a job he performed with élan and obvious grace. Mama had made the herring salad a day or two before, leaving out the customary beets, since they did not agree with her. Because I can no longer find the pale, thick asparagus that every self-respecting grocery stocked in those days among its canned goods, I also do not attempt the hollandaise sauce in which Mama drenched them for this and other special occasions. There were usually two cakes: Aunt Lina's sour cream chocolate and Aunt Melinda's lovely white angel food. Aunt Melinda, the newest member of the family, was also the innovator. Other parts of the meal might vary a little from one year to the next, but only she dared try something completely different. Even we little children were allowed some of the always red and rather sweet wine, though not much. Later we had "soda water" of the most innocuous fruit-flavored types, not an everyday beverage for us all in those days. I was never allowed to touch the heavily carbonated sorts reputed to contain stimulants that had caused some of the young people of the recent Jazz Age to positively destroy their health. Better wine than that, Mama said.

Since nobody was dressed for anything more active than going for a short walk, I wonder how all of us managed to enjoy those celebrations so very much. We were of several widely different age groups, so intricately related that I had to grow up before I could trace our connections with confidence, and we were isolated in that not-very-big house for half a day or more with little to entertain us. We did not even listen to the radio, much less have any real contests. The nearest thing to a competition was probably a comparison of one lady's crocheting with another's cut-work, or the men's attempts to blow smoke rings with their cigars. And yet the next day most of the same group assembled again, and from choice, although the excuse was always given

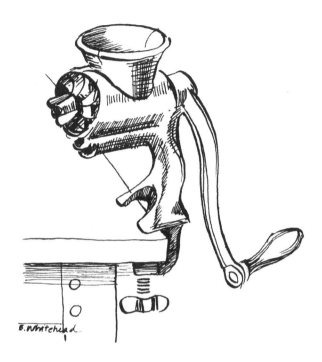

that we really must eat up the leftovers, since nobody had anything approaching enough room in any of the old iceboxes in the family. Iceboxes. Not electric refrigerators until somewhat later.

The next day, December twenty-sixth or "der zweite Weihnachtstag" (the second day of Christmas, literally), Oma's descendants would gather again, at Aunt Lina's, more often than not. I cannot think of a place more calculated to make leftovers appealing than her dining room: the large umbrella-shaped Tiffany glass shade suspended over the table, the gleaming sideboard built into the wall, and nicest of all—central heat! For this house had a cellar with a wood-burning furnace, later coverted to natural gas, and vents in the floor that kept every room comfortably warm, a rarity in older houses in south-central Texas then.

Aunt Lina's husband, whom my father and mother always called "Doctor," was the family dentist and, except for Oma, the only one of our entire local family who had come in from another area of Texas. A sensitive man, he always seemed to be suffering more than I did when he worked on my teeth. Perhaps it was to compensate for the unpleasantness of his profession that Onkel Carl was inclined to indulge in little extravagances so unlike the very modest entertainment my father permitted himself. In any case, Onkel Carl's family went on vacations that usually involved staying in resort hotels where, except for mixing with the other guests, resting and being waited on were the main entertainments. Our family took trips that always had instruction as part of the purpose, and our accommodations, though comfortable, were often of the most Spartan kind. Lurking in the background there was likely to be an exhibition or a museum to remind us that we would be edified by this vacation when we got back into our normal routine again. Onkel Carl, the only older member of the family who had attended college, even took his family along to professional meetings in big tourist meccas. In the dead of winter my father went with business associates to midwestern centers of industry, for which purpose he kept a very heavy overcoat in mothballs year after year. Papa brought back gadgets that were guaranteed to make even easier the simplest of chores or tricks he had learned at the magic shows that were one of his passions.

After dinner one particularly memorable second day of Christmas, Onkel Carl had some surprises of a different nature in store for us all. In the wide hall that bisected the house from front door to back there was an old upright piano with four pedals, one of which made the instrument sound like a harpsichord if one depressed it while playing. From the top of the piano

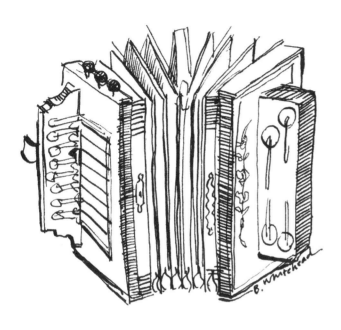

Onkel Carl took an accordion with numerous buttons and, to our consternation, played it quite expertly—polkas, drinking songs, the sort of thing accordions were invented for in the first place, presumably. To say that we were surprised is to put it mildly; we had not

known that he could play at all. Then, as if this were not enough, he handed the instrument to his aged mother, a gaunt woman even older than Tante Marie. She had just moved in with her son's family because of failing health, but she played with almost as much vivacity as he had shown, though she protested that she had not touched an instrument in years. I suspect it had been her Christmas gift the day before. Everything about that day was infused with magic, I began to think.

Then Onkel Carl shushed the women, who were discussing whether they ought to help the maid clear away the last of the dinner. We were invited back into the dining room and told to sit down, as Onkel Carl disappeared. A moment later he could be heard on the other side of the big sliding doors that separated the dining room from the parlor and that, mysteriously, had been shut when we arrived. The doors were pushed back ceremoniously into their pockets in the walls and there, in the parlor that had been cleared of almost all its usual furnishings except the Edison with its records a quarter inch thick, stood an enormous pool table that had never been there before. Invited to choose their cues, the men all started to chalk them as though they had spent all their lives in pool halls, though I am confident they had never played this game together, and I question that anyone of them knew the others knew how to play at all. As I observed this peculiarly masculine ritual that I had never seen before, I watched the gulf of years and formality that usually separated my imposing father from my shy brother fall away, recognizing that something extraordinary was happening. I wonder whether the two of them were aware of that metamorphosis, because it was so ephemeral that it could easily have escaped their notice, engrossed as they were in the game.

The game lost its appeal for the players late in the afternoon, but nobody seemed ready for the celebration to break up, with each household returning to its home and an early bedtime. When one of the young people—I forget which—suggested that tamales be sent in from a local Mexican grocer's, that departure from our traditional holidays struck everyone else as an inspiration. It was the first time Mexican food had ever been a part of our Christmas, though it was not to be the only time. It was, however, the last time we were ever all together in quite that way.

Minetta Altgelt Goyne
Arlington

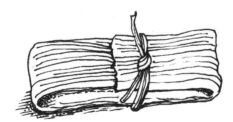

A West Texas Christmas Memory

Christmas in Texas is something that I should and do know a good deal about. As a now-advanced senior citizen, I have experienced many Christmases in my life, and every one of these, with the exception of three, has been spent in Texas. Those three times when I was an absentee were during and immediately after World War II when my Army Air Corps officer-husband was stationed in Colorado and California and when he was in graduate school in New York City. It was with deepest regret that we had to miss being at our Texas home for those three Christmases.

To Texans no season of the year and no day of the year are as stimulating, as exciting, or as important as the Yule Season and Christmas Day itself. Christmas customs may vary somewhat from person to person, depending upon family origin, location, and upbringing, but Christmas itself is universally loved in this state.

As a lifelong Texan, I am the daughter of parents who also lived their entire lives in Texas. And each of them was also from lifelong Texas families, one of which immigrated to the state before the Texas Revolution; the other came just at the close of the Civil War. Both of these families traced their ancestors, their lifestyles, and their customs back to pre-American Revolution immigrants who were English, Welsh, Scottish, and/or Scotch-Irish. Undoubtedly, many of our family practices, including Christmas customs, came down to us from these roots.

By the time I was born into the family, our principal Christmas customs had to do with several specific aspects of the holiday.

The Christmas Story

In our family, the children, of course, were taught the story of the birth of Jesus but not necessarily at Christmastime. We went to Sunday school and church services throughout the year, and we learned a great many Bible stories. It was always taken for granted that we understood and appreciated the Christmas story.

And, once implanted in us, it was left to be remembered and cherished. Nothing was ever done to dramatize or embellish it. There was never a crèche, either at home or at the church, and there was never a Christmas pageant. I was about seventeen years old before I ever saw a Christmas pageant, and then it was one that I myself produced.

The Christmas Tree

The Christmas customs in my family never seemed to me to have been begun by my parents but always impressed me as having been the practices which had been observed by their parents and grandparents. Year by year as our family grew in size and maturity, these customs remained the same—unless some unalterable circumstance dictated a necessary change.

In the matter of a Christmas tree, we followed the time-honored British and European use of an evergreen tree, freshly cut, and brought into the house to be decorated. During the early years of our family life, we lived in the piney woods of far East Texas and then in the mountains of far West Texas. There was never a problem about obtaining an evergreen Christmas tree. We took such a tree for granted—admired it, decorated it, touched it lovingly, and were ready to weep when the day came for that tree to be abandoned. Without a tree, it would not have been Christmas—could not have been!

Then my father's business necessitated that the family move from the mountains to the sand-hill country of West Texas. We loved the sand hills and spent hours sliding down the slopes, as if the sand were snow, and searching the crevices for flint-rock Indian arrowheads. And so the fall passed.

But when Christmas was approaching, we suddenly realized that there were no evergreens to serve as Christmas trees, none whatsoever! We were distraught; we were desperate. This was long before (as far as I know) there were artificial, manufactured trees available or before trees were trucked in from Colorado.

For days—weeks—we roamed the sand hills and the flat lands between them searching for something which could be converted into a Christmas tree. Finally, one day we stood and watched a tumbling tumbleweed blowing down the road near us, and we knew that tumbleweed would be our Christmas tree.

Exuberantly approaching the tumbleweed, we stopped its tumbling, carefully touching it to avoid its prickly thorns, and finally turning it over to get hold of its central root stem. Then we dragged it home with us and into our backyard. At first our parents were horrified at the idea of a tumbleweed Christmas tree, but, as always, they were admiring and supportive of their children's ingenuity and initiative. So eventually the tumbleweed was set up in our living room, decorated exactly as an evergreen tree would have been, and the family gifts were stacked around it.

The next year we became even more innovative. Not only one tumbleweed was used, but three, selected in graduated sizes to obtain a kind of triangular outline when stacked one on top of another.

During these evergreen-less years we also experimented a few times with a small mesquite tree but the mesquite had even sharper thorns than the tumbleweed. But we always had a Christmas tree!

Tree Decorations

Decorating a Christmas tree in the old days of Texas was by no means the simple matter that it is today. Ornaments and trimmings were difficult to come by, as well as expensive. Of course, we hoarded, from year to year, every single item which came our way that could be used at Christmas on the tree, but that was not enough. Much of our Christmas tree decoration was made at home.

Popped corn and fresh cranberries were the principal materials. First, we popped a large amount of corn. Then the family sat around for hours stringing (by the use of large needles) the white kernels onto long strands of white thread. Fresh red cranberries, if available at the grocery store, were also threaded onto long strands of red cotton. Then the strings of corn kernels and cranberries were draped around the tree to form garlands of Christmas glory. If available, candy canes were also hung on the tree limbs and any appropriate bauble on hand might be added. A homemade star cut from paper, wired to hold its shape and painted silver or gold, would be placed at the top of the tree. The stand was wrapped in a small rug or a scrap of fabric, and the tree was ready for Santa Claus.

Santa Claus

The Texas children with whom I grew up would never have questioned the existence of Santa Claus. From the poem "The Night Before Christmas" as well as from the tales of our parents, we knew all about this jolly old man. He lived (with Mrs. Santa Claus, my mother said) at the North Pole, where he and his elves worked industri-

ously all year long, making toys for the children of the world. On Christmas Eve, he always loaded his sleigh, hitched up his eight tiny reindeer (we even knew their names—Dasher, Dancer, Prancer and Vixen, Comet, Cupid, Donner and Blitzen) and off he would go, dashing around the world, stopping everywhere to leave presents for children. He certainly came faithfully to our house. Why should we have doubted him?

One year I had such a close encounter with Santa Claus that I never got over it. The year I was five we lived in the little town of Van Horn, Texas. As Christmas approached, I asked my father where he thought Santa Claus would "park" his sleigh when he stopped by our house. There was a high fence around the entire yard, but on the left side there was a large open space between the east door of the house and the trash barrels which stood against the back fence at the rear. It was this open space that my father suggested to me as the place where Santa would leave his sleigh when he came to our house to bring his gifts for us children. In the following days I looked out of the windows often at that space, picturing the scene as I thought it would look on Christmas Eve night.

When Christmas morning finally came, I found under the Christmas tree the gift Santa had left for me. It was a little play tea set with a small teapot, sugar bowl, cream pitcher, and six miniature cups and saucers. I was thrilled! I set up my little doll table and chairs, arranged the tea set, gathered my dolls, and we had a fine tea party.

After the excitement of the day had peaked, we children were put into our caps, coats, scarves, and mittens and sent outside to run about and relax in the fresh air. As I walked out of the east door into the open yard, I saw a box lying on the ground just about the place that Santa's sleigh would have stopped. I ran over and picked it up. It was the box that had originally contained my tea set. A picture of it was printed in color on the outside of the box and inside there were cardboard dividers obviously provided to form compartments for the various pieces of the little China set. Immediately, I knew what had happened. As he was about to depart, Santa had tossed his pack into the sleigh and the box, now empty, had dropped to the ground without him noticing it. So he had driven away and left it there. I could see it all vividly, and I treasured the incident during my entire childhood.

Claus presents. But I did not tell my younger brother and sisters about this revelation. After all, only a traitor would upset anyone's belief in good old Santa Claus.

Christmas Stockings

Today, when I visit friends and even relatives on the day before Christmas, I frequently see the stockings "all hung by the chimney with care, in hopes that St. Nicholas soon will be there." I notice, however, that there is a stocking for each individual in the family, including adults. This is not the way it was in my Texas childhood. In the "yester-years," only children hung up stockings. The practice ended somewhere between the years of finishing grammar school and graduating from high school. By then "kids" were supposed to be "young people," and Santa Claus did not come to see them. Another divergence is that today only one stocking per person is hung. In the "olden days" each child hung stockings, two of them—a pair. On Christmas Eve the children rummaged through their bureau drawers hunting out the nicest pair they possessed. These were brought to the Christmas tree or to the fireplace. The two stockings would be knotted

It was not until a number of years later that I realized that it was my father who had dropped that box as he was on his way to the trash cans after he and my mother had filled the stockings and set out the Santa

together at the top or pinned there with a large safety pin. The pair of stockings was then hung by the chimney or over the back of the child's own small chair or stool. Here Santa Claus would find and fill them.

In my Texas family there was a specific formula for stocking-filling. In each stocking was placed one apple, one orange, and, if available, one banana. If there were no bananas, an additional apple or orange was added. Between the fruit were handfuls of loose nuts (unshelled walnuts, pecans, peanuts, almonds, etc.), small packages of wrapped hard candies, and (after it became popular) even a package or two of chewing gum.

Each stocking also contained one or two small Santa Claus gifts—perhaps a little ball or horn, a small doll or stuffed animal or some other play toy. Finally, some fireworks were also pushed down into the deep stockings—a little package of firecrackers, a small box of sparklers, and one, two or maybe three fire rockets.

And sometimes when the filled stockings were returned to their place, a large candy cane might be hung from the center knot that kept the pair of stockings together.

Books as Christmas Gifts

Early in our childhood, the children in my Texas family learned that the most important Christmas presents we would receive from our parents would be books. This custom continued, year after year, until we were young adults. My very first two Christmas books were so dear to me that I have kept them all my life and recently had them re-bound at a cost of $73.50. The title of the oldest is *All Aboard for Fun.* Charmingly illustrated in color, it contains rhymes and jingles about the letters of the alphabet, the arithmetic figures from one to ten, the days of the week, the months and seasons of the year, and special holidays. From this book I learned a great deal before I even started school.

The second of my earliest childhood books was both more dignified and a great deal more serious. It was entitled *Sheaves of Gold,* and it contained some fourteen Bible stories from the Old Testament. Each was illustrated by a color print of an exquisite oil painting of a scene from the story. This book became the foundation of whatever knowledge of Biblical history I acquired as I grew up.

When the family had grown to the point of having several children to receive books at Christmas, it became the habit of our parents to give us sets of books—one set each year for all of us. In this way, my father and mother began to build a family library. This was very important because the towns we lived in were too small to have public libraries, and the school systems in Texas at that time were too poor to provide books. In those days, students had to purchase any and all of the books they used, including textbooks.

Sets of books given to us over the years (just to mention a few of the most loved and valued) included *The Children's Hour* (ten volumes published in 1907); *The Book of Knowledge* (twenty volumes given to us in 1919); *The World's Greatest Books* (twenty volumes given to us in 1922); *The Harvard Classics Shelf of Fiction* (twenty volumes, copyrighted in 1917 and given to us soon afterward); *John L. Stoddard's Lectures* (fifteen volumes published in 1923); and finally an all-important one-volume book, *Webster's New International Dictionary* which could not have impressed us more if it had been in fifty volumes because we were convinced that everything in the world we needed to know could be found in it.

Some of these books are still in my library shelves today, still usable and still used. But, above all, they are still loved and cherished as reminders of Christmases past.

Gift Wrappings

Today it may seem eccentric that such a trivial matter as Christmas gift wrappings could have become, in years gone by, a cherished Christmas custom. But that happened in my Texas family. Under the leadership of our mother, the paper, ribbon, cord and any other decoration were carefully removed and preserved for use again and again at future Christmases.

On Christmas morning the members of the family would gather around the Christmas tree to unwrap presents. Receiving one of the beautifully wrapped packages, the recipient would first just sit and look at it, enjoying its beauty and frequently saying, "It's too pretty to open." Then others would call out, "Open it! Open it!" So the owner of the gift would reach for a pair of scissors and, carefully studying the wrappings, would clip the ribbons or cord to preserve the bows and ties and also the long lengths of ribbons and cord. Then the same care would be taken in removing the paper wrappings. The package would be studied to see just how the paper had been folded around it; the paper would be carefully unfolded and slipped from the box it covered. (Scotch tape had not yet been invented!) It was unthinkable that anyone of us would have dared to snatch off the ribbons or tear off the paper wrappings and toss them into a wastebasket.

Once the wrappings had been removed, they were smoothed out, neatly refolded and placed in a safe spot until all the presents had been opened. Then our mother would bring in a large pasteboard box and everyone assisted her in laying the sheets of paper smoothly into it; on top of the paper, the ribbons were neatly arranged. My mother would then store this box carefully away.

The next year when Christmas was coming again, our mother would bring out the stored box of gift-wrappings. The ironing board would be set up and a warm iron provided. We pressed every sheet of paper and all the yards of ribbons. This done, we were now ready to get ready again for Christmas.

There are those who undoubtedly would consider all of this as strictly a matter of frugality. That may well have been part of it but I know in my heart that it was, at most, a minor part. We loved all those beautiful package wrappings and we wanted to use and re-use them as long as they were usable. And we did. To this day I cannot empty a wastebasket of torn and crushed Christmas wrappings without feelings of sadness and frustration.

Christmas Dinner

After the excitement of the Christmas tree, the family would settle down to a short period of quiet during which we re-examined, sorted, and enjoyed our gifts. Then it would be time to go to the kitchen to help our mother prepare the Christmas dinner. Of course, many preparations had already been made but there were always last-minute things to do. The turkey and dressing would be baking in the oven and other dishes would be waiting to be cooked.

When all was ready, the call to assemble in the dining room would resound. Gathering around the table, we took our places—my father at the head, my mother opposite him (but no one ever thought of that position as the "foot" of the table), the children and any guests present filled in the spaces along each side. When we were all seated, quiet fell upon us and we bowed our

Christmas Dinner
MENU
Baked Turkey and Cornbread Dressing
Brown Gravy
Candied Sweet Potatoes   Whole Cranberry Sauce
Waldorf Salad
Hot Rolls or Biscuits
Hot Tea or Coffee
Milk
Fruit Cake

heads. My father "said the blessing" or, as we sometimes called it "returned thanks." He used the simple words exactly as he spoke them at "everyday" meals: "Our Father, we thank Thee for these and all of Thy blessings. Amen."

Then talk flowed again, and my father stood up to carve the turkey. When he finished, he put a serving of turkey and dressing on each of the plates stacked in front of him and placed it to his right to be passed around the table. When everyone had a plate of turkey and dressing, the other dishes on the table were passed so that each could help himself or be helped to do so in the case of the children.

The Christmas dinner menu was traditional, exactly the same each year. No one would have ever thought, much less desired or tolerated, a change in it.

Christmas Cards

Christmas dinner over and the dining room and kitchen cleared, a signal was given for the family to reassemble in the living room. There we sat around in a semi-circle with my mother and father at the head of it. Mother would be holding in her lap a decorative basket or pretty tray, stacked on which would be many unopened envelopes. During the weeks preceding Christmas it was a strictly observed family custom to open no mail as it arrived if it bore the slightest resemblance to a Christmas card, Christmas note, or Christmas letter. These were carefully sorted out and set aside for this Christmas day ceremony. When we were all settled and ready, my mother would pick up at random one of the waiting envelopes, which she would open and immediately pass on to my father who would be seated on her right. My father would remove the contents from the envelope and tell us who it was from. Then he would read the messages enclosed— sometimes a Christmas card, sometimes a note or a letter. Finishing the reading, he would then pass the envelope and its contents to his right to be sent around the waiting circle and eventually returned to our mother. Then he would open another envelope and the procedure was repeated until all the Christmas mail had been enjoyed. This process might take an hour, an hour-and-a-half, or longer—we did not care. Loved ones were thought of, friendships refreshed, treasured memories revived.

Christmas Night Fireworks

Of all our Texas Christmas customs, none is so difficult for me to understand or to reconcile to our family background as our Christmas night fireworks. But it is true that the fireworks placed by Santa Claus in our Christmas stocking were not set aside for the New Year, much less the Fourth of July.

Christmas evening after everything else was over and just before the family was ready to retire, we all wrapped up against the cold and went out into our yard. There the sparklers were lighted, and we danced around the yard waving them rapturously. Then the firecrackers were exploded—bang! bang! bang! Finally, as the climax, one rocket at a time sent its blasts into space as we all stood motionless to watch the lights explode in the night sky. So Christmas in Texas ended, and we all went happily to bed calling to each other, "Merry Christmas to All, And to All a Goodnight!"

Freda G. Powell
Fort Worth

Remembering a Childhood Christmas in East Texas

I WAS BORN in East Texas and for eighteen years I spent every Christmas there. The swelling of emotions about Christmas was second to none in Tyler, Texas. The "square" downtown was decorated to perfection, and the attitudes of the people took on a Yuletide flair—people were unusually polite and kind to each other. The merchants' showcases displayed wintry scenes and a variety of traditional red, white, and green Christmas decorations. Aluminum icicles and fake snow finished off the decorations.

We were a poor family but our imaginations were not limited by our economic status. At home, a Christmas tree was literally cut down out in the country by my dad and hauled in a truck or tied securely on top of a car until it reached our house. The tree's base was built in our back yard by Daddy. I can still hear him hammering away at the crosspieces. Seldom did we have to do any shaping of the tree before it was placed in one corner of the living room. This is when and where the decorating began. First we made a homemade colorful chain-link garland from crepe paper and paste to swirl all around the tree. We made little ornaments from yarn and tin foil and hung them with some of Mother's green or dark sewing thread. Five-cent real candy canes were hung on the front side of the tree. Then, one of Mother's white sheets was carefully placed over the tree's base and crinkled up to resemble snow. Finally the only "store-bought" ornament—the shiny, silver star, was placed atop the tree. It was then finished.

Christmas Eve found the entire neighborhood busy as beavers cleaning house and beating the rugs, baking, shopping, wrapping gifts and hiding them in secret places. The gifts my brother and I had purchased for each other and for our parents were wrapped, usually in reusable tissue or construction paper, and placed under the tree just before we went to bed. Our gifts from our parents and grandparents were never wrapped at my house. This was mostly because of the lack of money to purchase the supplies, but I believe it was also because they wanted the surprise to be instantaneous. After all, who ever heard of Santa Claus having the time to wrap everybody's gift? Sometimes after we kids were in bed, trying desperately to go to sleep, our gifts were placed under the tree. The timing had to be right, otherwise curious and suspicious eyes could see and invalidate the existence of Santa Claus.

The aroma of fresh fruit, especially big delicious apples and grand sized oranges, swirled throughout the house. English walnuts, pecans, peanuts, and Brazil nuts filled little festive containers on the coffee table and end tables. A layered yellow coconut cake, caramel topped cake, chocolate cake, mother's favorite fruit cake, and sweet potato pies were carefully placed on the dining table and covered with a gauze-like cloth and then with a starched and ironed table cloth. The cornbread dressing, with its multiple ingredients, was placed in the refrigerator for "through" seasoning. The collard greens had been thoroughly washed, covered tightly in the cooking pot, and placed in the refrigerator. The chicken hen and other vegetables would be prepared early Christmas morning.

As soon as the light of day was felt on our faces Christmas morning, we were up and scrambling toward the Christmas tree to see what Santa Claus had left us. There was usually a toy for each of us, plus new clothes including sweaters and coats and other essentials such as socks and underwear. Each Christmas there was always a staple; our own personal little bag of ribbon candy, candy canes, bubble gum, and nuts. We were flying high with excitement over our presents.

Before breakfast, we had prayer and gave thanks for the birth of Jesus Christ. Breakfast on this special morning was non-traditional. Of course we had the usual pan sausage and biscuits, but this morning we could also have a small slice of cake or pie or whatever we wanted. Aromas from the dressing and chicken hens whetted the appetite for what was to come later.

Later, we dressed in our new clothes and took our traditional two-block walk to Mama Harris' house where we met up with the rest of the family on Daddy's side.

We usually carried one each of mother's cakes and pies for our contribution to the dinner while Daddy carried the present for Mama Harris. There we had fun enjoying my half-sisters and cousins and the new toys. We sang Christmas carols and other songs that were on the "pop chart" and played checkers and jacks while the grown folk sat around in the living room laughing and talking.

A short time after Christmas dinner, we headed for home, usually carrying samples of the desserts other family members had made. Once we were home, my brother and I continued playing with our new toys and modeling our new clothes. Occasionally, a neighbor or a church member would stop in sometimes carrying a basket of fruit or a paper plate containing a variety of desserts. Mother would prepare a "plate" for the guest made up of desserts she had prepared.

Finally, night was upon us and we were weary from the long day's events. We carefully folded away or hung up the new clothes. We put away the new toys, and we all went to bed early. Soon the house was silent.

Helen G. Green
DeSoto

Pleasing the Texas Palate

Pralines

Cook together, slowly, 3/4 cup milk and 2 cups sugar. Meanwhile, caramelize one cup of sugar in an iron skillet. When caramelized, stir into the milk-sugar mixture. Cook to soft-ball stage, stirring constantly. Cool to a lukewarm or barely warm temperature. Add 1 1/2 cups pecans and one teaspoon vanilla. Beat until creamy and drop on waxed paper.

Ann Gibson
Keller

Hoppin' John

After Christmas, New Year's is fast upon us, and Texas tradition dictates that you must eat ham and black-eyed peas on January 1 if you are to have good luck the year round. One superstition was that for every pea you ate on New Year's Day, you'd earn a dollar during the year. At that rate, you'd have to eat a lot of peas to pay your bills these days.

The black-eyed pea, not really a pea at all but a

legume or bean, is a humble food. The poorest farmer could always afford a pot of black-eyed peas. So people eat them on New Year's Day to show their humility and avoid incurring the anger of the gods. It's like asking God to be sparing with bad luck during the coming year.

Athens, Texas, calls itself the black-eyed pea capitol of the world and holds an annual Black-Eyed Pea Jamboree with a contest for the best recipe of the year. Maybe one year it was Hoppin' John.

How you eat your peas may depend on local custom and family habit—some like them cooked with hog jowl and served with cornbread. But some Texans, particularly those in the eastern part of the state, have adapted the Louisiana tradition of Hoppin' John, a stew-like dish that mixes black-eyed peas, ham, and rice.

It's hard to be specific about Hoppin' John. Like most traditional recipes, it has no definite amounts or ingredients, but you start with the peas and soak them overnight. Use about 8 cups of water for 1 lb. peas.

In the morning (maybe better do this on December 31), add one tbsp. Vinegar for every cup of peas, a good big ham hock, stewed tomatoes (cut up), chopped onion and celery, a little salt if you must, chili powder to taste. Other spices are optional: if you like your food hot, add a pod of red pepper; you might also try crushed basil, a bay leaf, garlic. Simmer the whole thing until the peas are tender—at least two hours.

Cook some rice separately, and serve Hoppin' John spooned over it.

There are probably as many versions of this recipe as there are cooks in Texas, but this is a basic start and leaves lots of room for individual experimentation.

In my family, we always called it Hoppin' Uncle John after a favorite uncle.

Judy Alter
Fort Worth

Sweet Potatoes

East Texas is sweet potato country. In fact, the town of Gilmer calls itself the "Sweet Potato Capitol" and holds an annual Yamboree in the fall, featuring a Yam Pie Contest. No self-respecting East Texan would omit yams from the Christmas Day dinner menu.

Sweet Potatoes and Bourbon

6 med. sweet potatoes   1/2 cup sugar
1 tsp. salt   3/4 stick butter
1 egg beaten   1/2 cup bourbon whiskey
dash nutmeg   marshmallows

Boil, peel, and mash potatoes; add sugar, salt, butter, and nutmeg. Beat egg into whisky and mix into potato mixture. Bake in casserole, topped with marshmallows.

Sweet Potato Pie Filling

3 cups boiled, mashed sweet potatoes
2 cups light brown sugar, firmly packed
6 eggs
1/2 lb. butter, melted
1 1/2 cup buttermilk
1 tsp. soda
1 tsp. vanilla
dash nutmeg

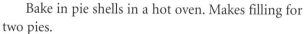

Bake in pie shells in a hot oven. Makes filling for two pies.

Linda (Mrs. Stephen) Butter
Longview

Fattigman's Bakkels
(also known as Poor Man's Cookies or Fry Cakes)

Fattigman's Bakkels are Norwegian Christmas cookies. This recipe was a favorite of Agnes Hanson who was of Norwegian ancestry. She married John Vinson Roach whose family was among the pioneers of Denton County. A Christmas tradition in the Roach home, marking the beginning of the holiday season, was making Fattigman's Bakkels after which the family enjoyed a cup of hot cider along with the crisp cookies.

3 eggs   2-3 cups flour
3 Tbsp. sugar   1/8 tsp. salt
3 Tbsp. milk or 3 Tbsp. sour cream
1/8 tsp. cardamom
1 tsp. vanilla
2 Tbsp. whiskey

Separate eggs, beating yolks slightly; beat whites until foamy but not stiff.

To yolks add sugar, milk or sour cream, vanilla, cardamom, salt, and whiskey.

Next, add whites of eggs and flour, as little as possible, to make soft dough; divide in half. Roll dough thin;

should be rubbery and spring back. Cut in diamond shapes and stretch out and cut slits in the center. Fry until light brown in deep hot lard at 375 degrees. Use lard only.

Dust with powdered sugar.

Jean Roach
Fort Worth

Buñuelos

Sometimes called Mexican Fried Cookies, these are traditionally served for Christmas breakfast.

1 tsp. ground cinnamon
l tsp. baking powder
4 cups flour
1/4 cup butter or oil or fat for frying
1 tsp. salt
2 tsp. sugar
1 cup water
sugar and cinnamon mixture

Sift all dry ingredients together. Slowly add water and a little oil. Turn onto a lightly floured board and knead until dough is smooth and elastic. Divide into about 40 small balls; roll out into approximately 4 to 6-inch circles. Fry in very hot oil (hot and deep) until delicately browned on both sides. Drain on paper towels and sprinkle with sugar and cinnamon mixture.

Taffy

1 cup light corn syrup
1 cup sugar
1 Tbsp. Vinegar
1 tsp. butter
Flavoring

Lightly butter a dish or platter. Combine, syrup, sugar, vinegar, and butter in a saucepan. Boil until firm, 252 degrees on the candy thermometer. Pour onto the dish. When cool enough to handle, add several drops of whatever flavoring you desire.

Then pull it.

The secret to making good taffy is to cool it quickly and then pull it properly. Ideally, the pulling should be done by two people, one to hold his or her hands in the position of a hook and the other to throw the elastic strip of taffy back and forth over the "hook." The more delicately the candy is handled, the lighter it will become.

Never twist taffy as too much air is lost that way. Instead, fold it back straight after each pull. The object is to get a whitish, porous condition by carefully stretching the candy and keeping it folded back upon itself. Remember to butter your hands first, so the taffy won't stick to your fingers. When the mass is fluffy and full of air, it will no longer have a plastic feel to it. Fold it into a long oval shape and lay the taffy on a smooth warm surface. Start rolling the right side of the oval with the heels of the palms of your hands. Roll into a thin rope. Cut or pinch off bite-sized pieces of taffy. Work quickly before the taffy hardens. Wrap in waxed paper to keep the candy fresh and store in tightly closed containers until ready to serve.

(Ernestine Linck and Joyce Gibson Roach, eds.
Eats: A Folk History of Texas Foods.
Fort Worth: TCU Press, 1989, 210)

Sugar Cookies

    1 cup sugar
    1 cup powdered sugar
    1 cup margarine
    1 cup cooking oil
    2 eggs
    4 cups plus 4 Tbsp. flour
    1 tsp. soda
    1 tsp. cream of tartar
    1 tsp. vanilla
    1/4 tsp. salt

Cream sugars, margarine, and oil until fluffy. Add eggs and vanilla and mix well. Add flour and other dry ingredients. Form dough into walnut-size balls and flatten with bottom of glass dipped in sugar. Bake at 375 degrees for 12 to 15 minutes.

35

Fudge

2 cups sugar
6 Tbsp. cocoa
3/4 cup milk

Cook very slowly to the softball stage. If you have a candy thermometer, the temperature will read 232 degrees. Do not stir the candy after it has reached the boiling point.

Remove from the heat and add 2 Tbsp. butter without stirring. Cool the candy at this point. Just let it stand. (Or put it in a pan of cold water if you want to hasten the process.)

When it is nearly cold, add 1 tsp vanilla. Now beat it vigorously until it is creamy and begins to lose its shine.

Add 1 cup chopped nuts and pour onto a greased platter.

Divinity

2 cups sugar
2/3 cup water
2/3 cup light corn syrup

Cook these ingredients quickly to 238 degrees on your candy thermometer or to the softball stage.

Whip 2 egg whites with a dash of salt until stiff. Pour the syrup over the eggs very slowly, beating all the time. When the syrup has been added, place the bowl holding the candy over hot water, or in a double boiler. Beat the candy until it sticks to the bottom and sides of the bowl and will stand in peaks. Remove it from the fire.

Add 1 1/2 tsp vanilla and 1 cup chopped nuts. Drop by the spoonful on waxed paper. At festive times, add chopped red and green cherries. Pecan or walnut halves are good, too.

Shaped Sugar Cookies

Cream together 1 cup sugar and 1 cup butter; add 1 egg and 1tsp. vanilla

Mix together 3 cups flour, 1 1/2 tsp. baking powder, 1/2 tsp. salt, 1/2 tsp. cinnamon, nutmeg, and allspice, and 1/4 tsp. cloves.

Mix the dry ingredients and add to the butter/sugar mixture.

Chill the dough for one or two hours; roll out the dough to about a quarter inch and cut it with a cookie cutter, any shape. Bake in a pre-heated oven at 350 degrees for 8 to 10 minutes.

Christmas Coffee Cakes

MY EARLIEST Christmas memories are of the coffee cakes my mother baked each Christmas Eve. She would bake early in the morning, and by the time my brother and I arrived in the kitchen—why was my father never a part of this?—ten or twelve tree-shaped cakes were ready to be decorated with gumdrops, red and green cherries, silver shot, red hots, red sugar, and whatever else entered our fancies.

Mother was quite strict about the decorating: she beat up sugar icing to just the right consistency—a little runny but not too much so—and then dribbled it across the cakes, with strict instructions to us on the order in which decorations had to go on.

Each finished cake was put on a square of cardboard—festively covered with aluminum foil!—and covered with clear wrap. By late morning, we were all off to deliver the cakes, and I think my father became part of the tradition here, though as soon as my brother was old enough to drive, the delivering was left to the two of us.

We had a regular list of recipients, and at every house where we stopped, we were assured that Christmas morning would not be the same without one of Alice MacBain's coffee cakes. We left a warning, the one every recipient already knew: don't put it in the oven to warm, because the icing will melt and the decorations all run off. And always, we left with hearty Christmas wishes ringing in our ears.

Newly married and living in Texas, far from my Chicago home, I began to make Christmas coffee cakes and soon had a list of friends who counted on them. When my father died and my mother moved to Texas, she once again took over the baking. When Mother failed and we had to move her out of her home, I carefully carried home the box that held coffee cake "decorates." And I told my brother, I truly felt I had inherited the family mantle.

Basic Coffee Cake Dough

> 2 pkg. granular yeast
> 1/2 cup warm water
> 1 can evaporated milk, plus enough water
>   to make 4 cups
> 1 scant cup vegetable oil
> 1 cup sugar

Dissolve yeast in tepid water (add just a pinch of sugar to help the yeast work) and let it rise about five minutes. Mix milk and water, shortening and sugar. Add dissolved yeast. Stir in enough flour to make a thin batter, the consistency of cake batter. Let this rise in warm place until bubbles appear on the surface.

Then, to one cup flour, add 1 Tbsp. salt, 1 heaping tsp. baking powder, 1 rounded tsp. baking soda; for Christmas cakes, we always add 2 tsp. cardamom and candied citron. Coat 16 oz. candied fruit with flour and mix into batter; if your family hates citron, you can substitute raisins (being a purist, I insist on citron, over the howls of my now-grown children, who don't like raisins either!)

Sift into first mixture. Keep adding flour until it is too stiff to stir with a spoon. Knead well. Don't let the dough get too stiff with too much flour or your coffee cakes will be heavy. This dough will keep a week or so in refrigerator.

To Shape Christmas Tree Coffee Cakes

Roll handful of dough into a log about 4-5 inches long and the size of your thumb (maybe a little bigger). Make the next roll a little shorter, and the next, and so on, until you end with a round-shaped piece of dough for the top of the tree. Add a round base for the trunk. Let rise until almost doubled in size.

To Bake

Bake at 375 for 20 minutes or until lightly browned. Cool thoroughly before decorating.

To Decorate

Make a basic powdered sugar/butter/hot water icing. Flavor as you like—I use vanilla and almond. Make the icing fairly runny—you want it to drip off the spoon, but not roll off the cake (tricky business, that!).

Line up all decorations before you begin. Put lighter decorations on first—silver shot, etc.—as they are more likely to roll off. You can always push quartered gumdrops or halved maraschino cherries into the icing.

I suggest any or all of the following:

green sugar or red (I like red better)

non pareils (those the little colored things— sort of multicolored shot)

silver or gold shot, if you can find it

red hots (these are particularly bad about rolling off)

halved red and green maraschino cherries

quartered gumdrops

anything else that strikes your fancy

Drizzle icing from a spoon over the cake in a back-and-forth motion. Then, quickly, apply decorations.

If you want warm coffee cake, heat it from the bottom only on a warming tray or a skillet on very low heat.

You can only make coffee cakes if you intend to share them with friends!

Judy Alter
Fort Worth

An Angel Unawares?

" .... **B**e not forgetful of strangers, for thereby some have entertained angels unawares." This from Hebrews 13:2 applies not to the physical but to the metaphysical, and if not to the metaphysical, at least to the unexplainable.

As a small child Uncle Bud Roark's niece lived with her family on a homestead claim some four miles northeast of a pump station of the Southern Pacific Railroad in Terrell County, Texas. Their abode was a one-room half dugout backed up against the south side of a hill.

The time was a Christmas Eve twilight. The year, 1903. Outside, Christmas cheer was spread everywhere in the form of a five-inch snow. Inside, yuletide joy fairly beamed from the bright, expectant faces of four children which, in turn, softened the work-and-worry lines seaming the faces of dad and mother.

As regards material signs of approaching Christmas, naught but

four somewhat-worse-for-wear stockings hung here and there.

As regards food, they were as close as they could possibly get to the traditional Christmas meal—fried venison with flour gravy, hot biscuits, homemade chow chow from last fall's tomato crop, red beans, and a slice of vinegar pie for dessert. The plain vanilla cake would taste mighty good, too, but it would have to wait until tomorrow—Christmas Day.

"Suppers on." This from mother triggered the usual quick but quiet stampede—two boys to the bench on their side of the table, two girls at their side, with dad at one end and mother at the other.

"Let us hear the blessin'." Dad's cue for bowed heads and still hands all around. "God our Heavenly Father, please accept our thanks for this, our daily bread. Amen."

A rap on the slab board door froze four small hands in mid-grab and brought an exchange of puzzled glances from dad and mother. Visitors to this long, lean, and lonesome land were few and far between, especially at this hour in this kind of weather.

It was a stranger seeking shelter for the night.

"Friend," said the father, "come in and have supper with us, and welcome. But as for staying the night—"

Here he paused, groping, hoping for the very softest of words with which to turn a cold and weary traveler from his door. "As you can see, the old sayin' 'Always room for one more' can't possibly apply here. But there is a place—"

"You mean the light?"

"Yes, the railroad pump station. They will put you up. If not to bed down, at least a place to sit by a roaring coal fire all night."

Supper, Uncle Bud's niece recalls, was a most memorable one. Already the presence of this tall, kindly stranger with the intense eyes was like a Christmas gift and then some. He was knowledgeable, he was mannerly, he was cultured, he was wise—a far cry from the occasional railroad hobo who passed their way. Better yet he was "lots of fun" as the children described him.

Long before the meal was over the family felt that the stranger's coming their way meant much more to them than it could have possibly meant to him. So when he arose from the table, patted each child on the head, and shook hands with the parents it was as if they were losing one of their own. Forever.

"I will walk you a ways," said the father, rising from his chair.

"By no means," said the stranger, pushing him back down. Though the man's voice was gentle, as was his gesture, the father got the message from those intense eyes. "I am the one with the warm coat," the stranger continued. "So, nobody beyond that door. Please." Then he was gone, his footsteps making crunching noises in the crusted snow.

So profound was the impression of this man that the children shed tears at his going, but they went right off to sleep. The tired mother pondered this most eventful occasion in her heart a long while before sleep would come, whereas the father tossed and tumbled the night through, his heart heavy and his conscience awry at having to turn this gentle stranger out into the frigid night.

Came the dawn—all this and Santa too! as each child eagerly emptied his stocking of an apple, an orange, a handful of Brazil nuts, and assorted candies, searching—in vain—for something more. After consoling each child as best she could, mother set about cooking breakfast while father went out to feed the work team and milk the cow. On the cow lot gate was attached a note, written in pencil, which read: "Be not forgetful of strangers: for thereby some have entertained angels unawares."

What was so unusual about that? Anybody could have written it. Maybe so. But not just anybody could have left without leaving tracks, especially since it had not snowed a flake since the storm blew over early yesterday afternoon! And surely he couldn't have—at least wouldn't have—backed out in the tracks he made coming in—which were still plainly visible.

Though seized with a feeling of deep, awesome wonder—to say the least—the father could not help but crack a wry grin. Would that an explanation were as simple for his wife—and for himself—as for the kids: "Simple. Why, the man caught a ride with Santa Claus!"

Paul Patterson
Crane

43

Three Hours of Snow in Texas

    Young hearts in Oak Cliff have always reached for snow
with flat panels of green and red felt
       glued to a glittered, curved craft stocking
     taped over the mantel of cardboard fireplaces with mocked fire
   flickering against the Christmas tree
   from the small ornamental bulb beneath the tin spindle
   balanced on a thin wire
      that rotates the spindle's fractured top of wavy slits
    to expose the heated bulb's light outward
beyond the shadows made by the corrugated flames and logs

    and the hearts want snow for Christmas
so without full thought   the mind's eye swallows that same hope

    maybe it is all the televised singing:
"Frosty…the snowman…was a jolly, happy soul"
or that reindeer tune where the red nose glows through the white night

    or maybe it was just the white faced singing of the now dead
their youth preserved   even until now
    Rosemary Clooney, Danny Kay…Bing Crosby and the brunette

44

all of them dressed in their version of hope and love and more Christmas
than is possible to ever have for this armpit of Texas

     and they are singing
convinced that if only the sky would bleed white for one night
     that all which is wrong in their lives on the road would be made right
     that if only   the back wall would open up into a white wall of snow
     even love among their pitiful lot would be possible
and so
     with their faces hurting   their mouths unleash a plea upon the annual viewing lot

     and they sing

and in Oak Cliff the small, brown-eyed faces
     lit alternately by the flickering lights of television and the H.L. Green department store fireplace
     believe it will come for them as well

and   they sing
 and their words are as much a list   to be checked twice
     to be rolled carefully and placed cautiously, unfurling beside the sugar cookies and milk
     left in the roach occasioned living room
as any such wish across the landscape of hope and time and wanted things
     left in the midst of Christmas Eves across the rest of the world
      and they sing

"Let it snow, let it snow…let it snow"
  just like they do on the television
"let it snow…I'm dreaming of a white Christmas…"
  but the next line falters in the collision of mouth and mind
   "just like the ones I used to know"

because
there is no such knowledge in Oak Cliff over an eight year span of Christmases
  and so the hope falters in the throat
      the brown, mind's eye cannot make it so
  for this family of young hearts

      but, there is one believer in all of Oak Cliff
    as the others fall away to the dark corners of sleep
having watched the stage door in the movie fall open to a sea of white flakes
    and the red lipped smiles breaking the actor's faces
he believes it all

and so,
  while the others feather themselves into bed sheets and pillowed dreams of "Who beast"

the Oak Cliff dreamer stands for an entire hour in front of the cardboard fire
  and rubs the heat of flickers into his bones
  with palms full of belief

he is warmed by this effort of the heart
and parades a too-warmed flannel pajama-ed backside around the adjusted living room
as the weather man breaks into the late-night program with news of early morning sleet
and he believes

and when the hours have passed and passed and passed
there is finally the chill of air chasing and claiming the early morning's breath

there is finally the sliding weight of rain
freezing and slipping into fits of colorless spit from the dark sky
as if an eraser banging cloud had been unleashed upon the blackboard of night

and soon it is falling…falling…falling
just like in the movie

and the dreamer croons his remembered lines anew
and deep within himself
as the snow begins to collect on the heads of shrubs and sills

he wants to wake the others
but the sun is breaking now behind the sky and times like this
are not to be wasted at bedsides and pulling at covers

so,
   with his birthday Polaroid in hand
  he dresses quietly and wades onto the screened porch
    only to find that the hour of falling has ended

  and the breaking sun has already started to claim back the Southern December greenery

so, he takes the picture
   frosty bush…whitened blades of grass…dalmation-spotted roof of the sedan

  and finally,
a penny's worth of snow ball
    balanced in the palm of his freezing, brown hand

now,
he can risk running to wake the others
   even if they delay and roll over into fits of disbelief and slumber

  he has the proof
leaning and coming into view
   resting there…right there…on the fireplace

Jas. Mardis
Dallas

Some Old-fashioned Gifts to Make

Christmas wreath pin

I or J crochet hook, green yarn, plastic ring, red ribbon, red glass beads

First make a slipknot. Put hook through the slip knot; then put the hook down through ring and draw thread from underneath and up through slipknot; chain five. Double crochet around the ring until tightly filled. Tie off and cut thread. Make a bow out of quarter inch or less red ribbon. Sew glass beads for berries. Use a medium sized safety pin for the back to secure on collar or yoke.

Cookie or treat box

Small oatmeal box, medium to heavy Christmas wrapping paper, Elmer's Glue and water

Cut heavy Christmas wrapping paper to fit around an oatmeal box. "Paint" a thin layer of half Elmer's Glue

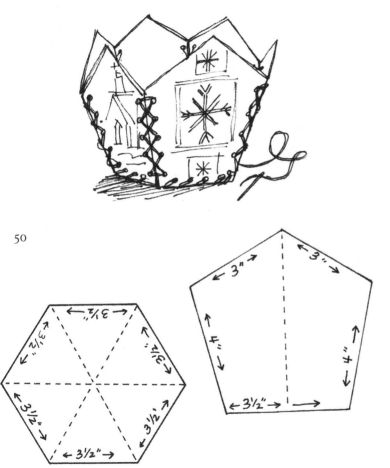

and water around box. Affix paper to box. Press the lid lining out of top and repeat paper and glue process. Replace liner. Fill the box with sugar cookies. Use a 3-inch biscuit cutter for the cookies so they will be small enough to fit loosely into the oatmeal box.

Card or treat basket

6 Christmas cards (5 x 7 size), crochet thread,
extra large needle with large eye

Using the templates provided, cut 6 of #1 for sides. Cut 1 of #2 for bottom of basket. Open this cards since the #2 template is too large for folded cards. The inside bottom can be covered with a doily or paper after the basket is completed to conceal the unmatched pattern. Using crochet thread and large needle, join the sides together using blanket stitch. (You may also use a quarter inch paper punch if the needle proves too difficult for young hands; however, the needle gives the basket a more finished look.) Then attach the sides to the bottom using the same stitch. Put Christmas cards inside the basket or use it for a batch of cookies or candy to give to friends.

The Cowboys' Christmas Ball

In the mid-1880s, a young reporter for The New York Times, *Larry Chittenden, arrived in Anson, Texas, and took a room in the Star Hotel, just in time for the first Cowboys' Christmas Ball. Chittenden was so intrigued by watching the couples dance, performing such traditional dances as the schottishe, heel and toe polka, waltz, and Virginia reel, that he wrote a poem about the event, the now-classic "Cowboys' Christmas Ball." The poem was first published in 1890 in the* Anson Texas Western *and then appeared in 1893 in* Ranch Verses, *a collection of Chittenden's work.*

The dances were held irregularly for several years until 1934. After that, Anson dancers, who followed the old dance customs, steps, and songs, were invited to folklore festivals and once danced on the White House lawn. The group incorporated in 1937, and in 1940 a permanent home—Pioneer Hall—was built for the ball. It is now a three-day event held before Christmas each year, bringing visitors from all over the United States. The frontier atmosphere and pioneer dance routines have been preserved.

'Way out in Western Texas, where the Clear Fork's
    waters flow,
Where the cattle are "a browzin'," an' the Spanish ponies
    grow;
Where the Northers "come a-whistlin'," from beyond the
    Neutral strip;
And the prairie dogs are sneezin', as if they had "The
    Grip";
Where the cayotes come a howlin' 'round the ranches
    after dark,
And the mocking-birds are singin' to the lovely "medder
    lark";
Where the 'possum and the badger, and the rattle-
    snakes abound,
And the monstrous stars are winkin' o'er a wilderness
    profound;
Where lonesome, tawny prairies melt into airy streams,
While the Double Mountains slumber, in heavenly kind
    of dreams;
Where the antelope is grazin' and the lonely plovers
    call—
It was there that I attended "The Cowboys' Christmas
    Ball."

The town was Anson City, old Jones's county seat,
Where they raised Polled Angus cattle, and waving
    whiskered wheat;
Where the air is soft and "bammy," an' dry an' full of
    health,
And the prairies is explodin' with agricultural wealth;
Where they print the *Texas Western*, that Hec McCann
    supplies,
With news and yarns and stories, uv most amazin' size;
Where Frank Smith "pulls the badger" on knowin' ten-
    derfeet,
And Democracy's triumphant, and mighty hard to beat;
Where lives that good old hunter, John Milsap from
    Lamar,
Who "used to be the Sheriff, back East, in Paris, sah !"
'Twas there I say, at Anson, with the lively "Widder Wall,"
That I went to that reception, "The Cowboys' Christmas
    Ball."

The boys had left the ranches and came to town in
    piles;
The ladies—"kinder scatterin'"—had gathered in for
    miles.

And yet the place was crowded, as I remember well,
'Twas got up for the occasion, at "The Morning Star
    Hotel."
The music was a fiddle, an' a lively tambourine,
And a "'viol come imported," by a stage from Abilene.
The room was togged out gorgeous—with mistletoe
    and shawls,
And candles flickered frescoes, around the airy walls.
The "wimmin folks" looked lovely—the boys looked
    kinder treed,
Till their leader commenced yellin': "Whoa ! fellers, let's
    stampede."
And the music started sighin', and awailin' through the
    hall,
As a kind of introduction to "The Cowboys' Christmas
    Ball."

The leader was a feller that came from Swenson's
    Ranch;
They called him "Windy Billy," from "little Deadman's
    Branch."
His rig was "kinder keerless," big spurs and high-heeled
    boots;
He had the reputation that comes when "fellers shoots."

His voice was like a bugle upon the mountain's height;
His feet were animated, an' a *mighty, movin' sight.*
When he commenced to holler, "Neow fellers, stake yer
    pen!
"Lock horns ter all them heifers, an' russle 'em like
    men.
"Saloot yer lovely critters ; neow swing an' let 'em go,
"Climb the grape vine 'round 'em—all hands do-ce-do!
You Mavericks, jine the round-up—Jest skip her water-
    fall,"
Huh ! hit wuz gettin' happy, "The Cowboys' Christmas
    Ball!"   53

The boys were tolerable skittish, the ladies powerful
    neat,
That old bass viol's music *just got there with both feet!*
That wailin', frisky fiddle, I never shall forget;
And Windy kept a singin'—I think I hear him yet—
"O Xes, chase your squirrels, an' cut 'em to one side,
"Spur Treadwell to the centre, with Cross P Charley's
    bride,
"Doc Hollis down the middle, an' twine the ladies'
    chain,
"Varn Andrews pen the fillies in big T Diamond's train.

"All pull yer freight tergether, neow swallow fork an'
    change,
"'Big Boston' lead the trail herd, through little
    Pitchfork's range.
"Purr 'round yer gentle pussies, neow rope 'em! Balance
    all!"
Hugh! hit wuz getting' active—"The Cowboys'
    Christmas Ball!"

The dust riz fast an' furious, we all just galloped 'round,
Till the scenery got so giddy, that Z Bar Dick was
    downed.
We buckled to our partners, an' told 'em to hold on,
Then shook our hoofs like lightning, until the early
    dawn.

Don't tell me 'bout cotillions, or germans. No sir 'ee!
That whirl at Anson City just takes the cake with me.
I'm sick of lazy shufflin's, of them I've had my fill,
Give me a frontier break-down, backed up by Windy
    Bill.
McAllister ain't nowhar! when Windy leads the show,
I've seen 'em both in harness, and so I sorter know—
Oh Bill, I sha'nt forget yer, and I'll oftentimes recall,
That lively gaited sworray—"The Cowboys' Christmas
    Ball."

Larry Chittenden

The Cowboys' Christmas Ball

A Short Story

"Y OU'LL not go dancing, Ellsbeth," Papa thundered, his eyes peering out at me from under bushy eyebrows. Papa was the minister in Anson, Texas, and he frowned on all kinds of dancing, even the Anson Cowboys' Christmas Ball which had now, by 1895, become an annual event.

"Papa . . . please, just for the Christmas Ball?" I was ashamed to be begging, but I'd set my heart on going to that dance. "One last fling," I'd told my good friend, Harriet Stedman, "before I marry Edward Greenough."

"You're promised to Edward," Papa said in his preaching tone of voice, "and you'll not be dancing with other men."

"But Edward is away . . . ." I faltered.

He turned back to his desk, where he was working on his Christmas sermon. No doubt, I thought bitterly, it will be about the evils of worldly pleasures.

"I . . . I can't go without you," Harriet said when I told her Papa's command. "I don't have the nerve." Harriet was plainer than me. No one had to tell me that next to her I looked the town beauty. It was mostly because Harriet was more than a little too fat and wore her pale brown hair pinned too close to her head. I prided myself on a tiny waist, shapely arms and shoulders if I did say so, and wonderful red hair that I'd inherited from my mother. I wore it pulled back but loose enough that the curls showed. Papa warned me frequently about the perils of vanity.

"Bother the nerve," I said. "How can you pass up the chance to dance and dance all night?"

"How can you pass it up?" she countered, her look turning thoughtful. "You could still go," she suggested. "You could pretend to go to bed early."

At first I was horrified at the idea of lying to Papa, but I quieted my conscience by reminding myself that it was my last fling before getting married. Edward would surely understand, and Papa would never know. And so we made our plans.

Dinner that evening was endless. Mama had roasted a chicken and made her fluffy mashed potatoes, with light biscuits and homemade preserves. She even made bread pudding, my favorite, but I only picked at it and said my head ached slightly.

My younger brother, Teddy, played with his food, making Papa angry enough to issue a stern warning, while Mama said gently, "Now, James, your temper . . . ."

"Tonight's the Cowboys' Christmas Ball," Teddy said, pushing another forkful of potatoes around in the gravy. At twelve, he was all the things I didn't want in a brother—loud and nosey and mean, looking for ways to get me in trouble. If Teddy found out about my plan, I was done for.

Finally, dinner was over, the dishes done. "I believe I'll go to my room early," I said, feigning a yawn.

Mama and Papa exchanged looks, but I think they attributed my fatigue and headache to disappointment about the dance.

Once I was excused, I ran to my room and quickly freshened my hairdo, put just a tiny bit of forbidden color on my cheeks, and a dab of vaseline on my eyelashes to make them shine. Then I laced myself into my best corset, put on a petticoat, threw an old wrapper on over all, and climbed into bed. There was no danger I'd fall asleep—excitement and anticipation had me at such a fever pitch I could scarce lie still.

At last, Mama came tiptoeing in the room, as I had known she would, to kiss me gently and murmur, "Sleep tight, Ellsbeth."

She had barely closed the door before I was out of bed like a coiled spring. I stuffed my pillows into shape under the blankets, so that it looked at a glance as though I were fast asleep. Then, oh so carefully, I put on my best silk taffeta dress—it was a blue, the color of a cloud-free sky—and wrapped myself in a deep gray wool shawl. There was no way I could check my appearance in the mirror, for I dared not light a lamp. No matter—I felt beautiful.

By the time Harriet knocked on the window, I was ready, my heart in my mouth from a strange mixture of excitement and fear. The minute I opened the window, I heard the fiddlers warming up at the hall where the dance was held. My feet itched to be dancing.

The hall was crowded with people I'd never seen before. Cowboys from ranches far and near had come, and ladies had gathered from miles away. Here I saw Bertha Williams and there Joseph Mulroney but not many townsfolk. This was truly a cowboys' ball. The hall, decorated with mistletoe and Christmas ribbons and candles that flickered from around the walls, seemed the most festive—and forbidden—place I'd ever been.

The music began—a fiddle, a tambourine, and a bass viol—and the leader, a man called Windy Billy from Swensons' Ranch, called for everyone to take their partners. A cowboy, whose clothes and hair looked to be mostly clean, grabbed my hand, and soon we were swinging right and allemanding left with the others. "Salute

your lovely ladies; now swing an' let 'em go," called Windy Billy. The dancing was fast and furious, until I felt downright giddy. When at last the music stopped, I nearly fell against my partner, who bowed self-consciously and thanked me kindly for my company.

I made my way to the punch bowl and there I saw him—a cowboy so different from all the others that I caught my breath suddenly. He wore black from head to toe, even the proud and new Stetson on his head. His pants fit neatly rather than bagging like those of most of the cowboys, and his shirt looked to have been carefully pressed. The only spots of color about him were a silver belt buckle and a red bandanna about his neck.

He saw me at the same time and smiling ever so slightly raised his punch glass in salute. Flustered, I smiled back and turned to get my punch. In an instant he was at my side. "Allow me," he said, reaching for a glass and pouring me just the tiniest bit of punch. "I doubt you'll want more than this, ma'am. Some lowlife has put spirits in this punch, and I would not think that a lady of your type . . . ."

Spirits! "Oh, no sir, I could not touch it."

"Perhaps a sip of water," he said. "I know where the

barrel is." In seconds he was back with a glass of cool clear water, the best I had ever sipped.

"You . . . are you from a neighboring ranch?" I asked.

"No, ma'am, just passing through. But I heard the music and couldn't miss a fine dance." His eyes looked into mine at every word, and I could not tear my gaze away. Vaguely I wondered what had happened to Harriet and then decided I couldn't worry about her.

The music struck up again, and Windy Billy called for another dance. "May I?" the cowboy asked, and I nodded, taking his arm to head for the floor.

"Down the middle, an' twine the ladies' chains.

Pen the fillies in the big Diamond T train,

All pull your frieght together, now swallow fork an' change,

Purr round your gentle ladies, now rope 'em! Balance all!"

Windy Billy called dance after dance with no rest for the wicked, until at last I was panting for breath in a most unladylike way. I knew my hair flew about my head and my face glistened with perspiration. We had said not three words since the dancing began, but there was an electricity between us that confounded me. I had never known a man could make me feel so . . . so . . . so wonderful!

"Shall we take a breath of air?" my companion asked.

I looked carefully about the room but saw no sign of Harriet anywhere. She had probably gone home in a huff, I decided. "I . . . I must be going," I said.

"I'll escort you. Can't have a lady walking home alone this late at night."

Outside the frosty air was a welcome change from the sweaty stuffiness of the dance hall. Without hesitation, my cowboy—he had become "my cowboy" even though I didn't know his name—took my arm, wrapped it into his arm, and then clasped a firm hand over mine.

"You," he said, "are about to be married to someone you don't love."

Indignantly I tried to pull away but he held my hand firm. "Of course I love Edward. How did you know anyway?"

He chuckled. "I can tell. And you don't really love Edward. You're gonna' have a dull, ordinary life with him. Why don't you come away with me?"

"Come away with you?" I asked in amazement. "I don't even know your name!"

"It's Chance," he said, laughing again, and "that's what you'd be taking—a great, big chance. But I'd show you how to ride like the wind and dance till you dropped, and I'd buy you diamonds and rubies and silks and satins. You'd never scrub a floor or cook a meal a day in your life!"

"Go on with you," I said. "You're not the King of France!"

"No," he said, "but I've my own kingdom . . . and I'd like to share it with you."

Edward's face swam before my eyes. Dear, dull Edward, dedicated to his bank, determined to be a useful citizen, not an ounce of adventure in him. I swept my hand before my eyes as though to banish Edward's presence, and Chance laughed aloud again. Then he stopped, suddenly, and, turning me toward him, bent his head to kiss me.

His was not the mushy kiss I'd come to expect from Edward. It was strong, demanding, so intense that I felt almost a pain shoot through my insides and end tingling down one leg.

"See?" he said. "We'd be king and queen, no matter where we were."

"Where would we go?" I asked, knowing that I could never run away with this man and yet longing beyond all reason to do one adventuresome thing in my life.

"Anywhere you want," he said, "but if you say no, you'll never see me again."

That seemed harsh. "Surely, you could come through Anson from time to time."

"I can't," he said shortly, "and I won't." Then his voice lightened. "Besides, you'll be married to Edward."

When we reached my house, I had to explain about the window, and he got a last good laugh from boosting me up so that I could climb quietly back in, with me cautioning him all the while to be quiet lest he wake Papa. I turned, meaning to reach down for one last kiss, but he was already headed away. He stopped, only briefly, to turn and wave.

"Have a good life," he called.

Next morning Mama had to call me three times for breakfast, and Papa remarked that I must not have slept well.

"Does your head still ache?" Mama asked carefully.

No, I wanted to answer, but my heart does.

Just then, Teddy rushed in from the barn where he'd been sent to pitch hay for the horses. "Look what I

59

found," he shouted, waving a knotted red bandanna in his hand. "Looks like someone slept in the barn," he said. "The hay has the shape of a man pressed into it . . . a tall man."

"Give me that bandana," I said, almost grabbing it from his hand.

He danced away, holding it aloft. "What makes you think it's for you?"

"I . . . I think I recognize it," I said hesitantly, wondering how I would explain that to Papa.

"Give me the bandana," Papa said quietly.

"It's . . . there's a note. It's for Ellsbeth."

"Then give it to her."

Obediently, Teddy handed me the bandanna. The note said, "Keep this for luck . . . for you and for me." I undid the knot and pulled out a shining gold coin.

"I heard there was a bank robbery out to Sweetwater night before last," Papa said. "Looks like that might be some of the gold that was stolen." Then he left the room.

"I never did have to explain that bandana or the gold coin to Papa, though Teddy badgered me something fierce to tell him the story. I didn't even tell Harriet . . . and I surely never mentioned it to Edward. But I kept the gold coin, and every Christmas I would get it out and finger it and wonder what had happened to Chance. I wished him luck."

"Did it bring you luck?" The young woman who'd been sent to the county home to visit the old folks at Christmas had listened to the story in amazement.

"You might say that. I married Edward Greenough, and we raised five strong sons. Two of 'em gone now, and Edward's been gone some thirty years . . . but we had a satisfactory life.

"But I didn't keep that gold piece for luck," I said. "I kept it for the memory of what might have been."

Judy Alter
Fort Worth

Bilingual Whirl

"IMAGINE a morning in late November." So begins a favorite holiday book at our house, Truman Capote's *A Christmas Memory*. When seasonally I suggest that we read it aloud, my daughter, Libby, says, "You know you can't read it without crying, just like I can't get through *Emmet Otter's Jug-Band Christmas*." The magic of words: reading, writing, and remembering. Comfortable in front of a fire, I re-read Capote's story to help me journey back on the river of memory, back to my hometown of El Paso, Texas; the desert space where I was both a child and a parent. The memories intertwine, as memories do.

Was I first smitten by Capote's story in print or when I saw the television production with Geraldine Page as his eccentric sixty-ish cousin, "each other's best friend." Capote, the young narrator, has perfect pitch. His cousin captured my heart as she'd obviously snagged his. Is it that she reminded me of my aunt, also old enough to be my grandmother, of the shining spirit within such intense, generous women?

And if spirits shine daily, then during the Christmas season, they glow irrepressibly, at least they did at our rock house. My three siblings and I enjoyed years when we had an adult per child at 704 Mesita Street. Two parents, Mamande, our maternal grandmother, and our aunt whom we called *Lobo,* which, as you probably know, means wolf. Our aunt called us her *lobitos,* her wolf-cubs, and she became *Lobo* to us and our friends. Interesting how we become a name, hers connoting fierce love and protection. These four adults expressed their affection with ease in both English and Spanish, with winks and *abrazos,* a daily assumption on our part. Holidays only increased the intensity of our expectations.

"What do you remember about Christmas when we were little?" I ask my sister Stella.

"Leaving milk and cookies for Santa and running in on Christmas morning to see if he'd come."

"Oh, yes, I say. "The cookie crumbs."

"Crumbs? No wonder I got better gifts than you did," she says engaging in the popular sibling game, "I Got More and Better."

I start laughing when I realize that when her words created the scene of a treat by the chimney for Santa, I time-traveled from our childhood home to the home on La Cadena where I raised my three children. In a matter of seconds and without moving an inch, I traveled twenty-five years from child leaving the cookies to parent eating them and leaving some obvious crumbs before filling red stockings.

When I was young, Christmas and New Years meant trips across town to visit Lita, my paternal grandmother, who spoke only Spanish. How my father savored her tamales, *menudo,* and drinking warm, thick, *champurrado.*

"Honey, taste this. Taste this," Daddy would say. "It's just great." And to his mother, *"Rico, mama, pero rico."* My siblings and I shivered at the word tripe connected with *menudo* and soon retreated to the sweet tamales tasting of raisins, cinnamon, anise, and the cookie *animalitos.*

"What do you remember about Christmas at our house, Unks?" I ask Uncle Lalo, now eighty-five.

"Let me get my memories going," he chuckles. "They're slower now."

"We'd go to Midnight Mass at St. Patrick's Cathedral," I say, "and I'd struggle to keep my eyes open." My father was a Knight of Columbus, so perhaps those nights he'd have worn the formal black suit and carried a sword at church. We thought our tall dad looked simply splendid.

Speaking to my uncle, I have a vague recollection of going to Las Posadas, when I was little, long before Mamande, who also spoke only Spanish, came to live with us. *Posada* means inn, and this tradition is a re-enacting of Mary and Joseph's journey as they searched for lodging, a place for Mary to give birth. For nine nights, a group journeys from house to house praying, singing. My grandmother would take me with her to the home of her friend so devout she had a chapel in her home.

My uncle easily recalls the details. "Señora de la Torre had a large home with sliding doors between some of the rooms," he says. "First, we'd all go to her chapel and say the rosary, in Spanish, of course. Then part of the group would go behind doors and play the part of the inn keepers, and part of us would sing the roles of Joseph and Mary. How did that song go?"

Together in our squeaky voices, Uncle Lalo and I sing, "*¿Qui-én les da-apos-a-a-a-a-da?*" "Who will give them room?"

"The de la Torres owned a wholesale company,"

Uncle Lalo says, "so each night after the prayers and singing, we'd go to a large back room, and they'd serve oranges and candies." I can well imagine how my grandmother would have bundled me up for the walk back to her house, taken my mittened hand and held it tightly saying, "*Vamos, Patricia. Vamos.*"

"Your aunt and I would spend Christmas day at your house," says my uncle. "I don't remember the details, but the four of you were running around with your gifts, and everything was happiness."

"The tree was by the arched front window," I say.

"And it looked so pretty from outside," he says. Although we're talking by phone, he and I journey back there together, on words.

"That's what I remember too, the happiness," I say, seeing the living room on Christmas morning full of boxes, bikes, books, wagons, dolls, stereos, hearing Bing Crosby singing, "I'm dreaming of a white Christmas," as we said, "*¡Mamande, ven a ver!*" asking our white-haired, quiet grandmother to come and see what treasure we'd received.

In both backyards, my children's and my childhood one, some Christmas mornings meant a swing set, a slide. Imagine the December morning Mom said,

"Bundle up and go see what's out back." Through the windows, we saw a square made of wooden planks connected to a center axis. We rushed out and realized the device spun. "A merry-go-round!" we four chimed discovering that we could run along the sides, push our magic ride faster and faster, and then jump on. We flew!

"*¡Lobo! ¡Mamande! ¡Mira, Mira!*"

My memories, like my life, a bilingual whirl.

Pat Mora
Santa Fe, New Mexico

64

Christmas Customs Then and Now

CHRISTMAS in Texas has remnants of much of the folklore and religious customs of Europeans. In olden times the celebration took place on Christmas Eve and centered on the crèche. Later, the Germans originated the custom of having the Christmas tree and gifts from Saint Nicholas on Christmas Day. The French began their celebration on Christmas Eve and continued through January sixth, the feast and giving of gifts to coincide with the arrival of the Wise Men in Bethlehem.

Today children leave a plate of cookies, some candies, and a glass of milk for Santa Claus. This is like an old Swedish custom of setting out a meal for the spirits to enjoy while the family is away at church.

The custom of having roast pig—a meat popularized recently in Texas communities, where a Feast of Carols is presented along with a traditional English Christmas feast—is derived from Scandinavian countries. Brought into the great hall garnished with an apple in its mouth, it was an offering to the Norse Goddess Frey to induce successful crops for the coming year.

The Christmas tree too was a sacrificial token. The family would select a fruit tree during the bearing season, the most beautiful and bountiful tree in the fields. It would be marked and, for Christmas, cut, brought into the house and decorated for the festivities. Today we have fruit-like ornaments for the trees. And an orange in the stocking is a symbol of nature's bounty when the gods are appeased.

Oranges in early Texas were a rare treat—hard to come by and costly. There might be no gifts under the tree, but a luscious, juicy orange for each child was a piece of gold in the toe of a Christmas stocking.

The fruitcake is yet another offering to the gods of fertility to insure good harvests. The more fruits, the more pleasing to the gods. And there must be currants, for the grapevine is a sign of peace and plenty.

After the gifts and the midday feast, there is visiting. People of English heritage say that for every cake tasted in a friend's house on Christmas Day, a month will be added to your life.

65

(Ernestine Linck and Joyce Gibson Roach, eds. *Eats: A Folk History of Texas Foods.* Fort Worth: TCU Press, 1989, 195-196)

The Christmas Ball at the Matador

IT WAS in 1879 that Henry Campbell sent for his wife, Lizzie Bundy Campbell, who had remained in Ellis County while he went West searching for ranch land. When she joined him at Ballard Springs, he was living and batching in a dugout. She said, "No thank you, I will not live underground." So he hurriedly found a tent that they lived in until he could get lumber for a house. Theirs was the first wooden house built in that area, and because it was painted white and surrounded by a white picket fence, it became "The White House."

The first Christmas the Campbells lived in "The White House" was to begin a beautiful tradition that lasted off and on at the Matador for almost seventy-five years. Lizzie Campbell started preparing for this holiday in November, even ordering Christmas tree decorations from Fort Worth—which arrived in March. She was a superb hostess, thoughtful and ingenious. She also included in her invitation to the celebration cowboys, not only of their ranch, but as far away as the Spur Ranch, neighbors (the nearest one at that time was twenty-two miles away), travelers, and anyone who needed a home to observe Christmas. The tree was decorated with home-made candles, popcorn strung on wire or string, and odds and ends.

For the feasting, Mrs. Campbell cooked for days and days. Among the foods were wild turkeys, larded liberally with strips of bacon which came from wild hogs on the range, cornbread dressing, boiled hams, venison steaks, a huge pot of antelope stew with dumplings (which the cowboys called "sinkers"), wild rice, corn pudding, apple pies from dried apples, and a "washtub" full of doughnuts. Popcorn balls were made from the popcorn she had brought from Ellis County, and which the guests ate all during the festivities.

Some fiddlers were found among the cowboys, and three of these provided music for the dancing. However, it is said that their repertoire was rather limited. The dancing lasted all through Christmas Eve and started again on Christmas night, and until daylight the following day. This was the beginning of a great and memorable tradition—The Christmas Ball at the Matador.

One of the wives who continued the tradition, as well as entertaining for many other important occasions, was Pauline, the wife of Maurice J. Reilly, while he was superintendent at the Matador division from 1923-1946. Her preparation and performance was, of course, made to fit the times and customs of a different age, but the legacy of the first Christmas on the Matador was always in the minds of the participants.

Hortense Sager recalled the Christmas ball that began the festivities on Christmas Eve with guests coming from far and near to join the celebration.

Decorating the tree was a big part of the occasion; this part was made more joyful after the guests had partaken generously of her bourbon-rum ice cream pie and a "spot" or two of old-fashioned syllabub.

For Christmas dinner Hortense served what came to be known as a Sager specialty, oyster salad, a cross between a cold dressing and a relish, always served with the roast turkey. Other foods for the dinner were beef roasts, an assortment of salads and vegetables, and cakes and pies of every type and kind.

After the Christmas Eve tree decorating and after much jubilation and gaiety, someone would watch to see if departing guests would find the cattle guard at the gate opening that led onto the road. Yes! Some missed it.

Some Matador Christmas Recipes

Bourbon Christmas Pie
Prepare one baked pie shell ahead. Mix 1/2 cup bourbon and 2 tablespoons rum into 2 pints softened vanilla ice cream. Stir in 1/2 cup mincemeat and pour into shell. Freeze. Before serving, spread with sweetened whipped cream.

Syllabub
Syllabub is closely related to eggnog, although eggnog calls for strong liquor and syllabub traditionally has been made with wine, making it what many once thought of as a ladies' drink. It is most often served at Christmas time with cookies and is mild enough for children to drink. As with many other recipes, there are many versions of syllabub. There is a thick version served in dishes as a dessert, and a thin version served as a drink. Then there is an old recipe that says, "put a bowl with some wine under a cow and milk the cow into the bowl until a fine froth has formed at the top, then drink." And still another version that says, "sweeten a quart of cider with refined sugar and a grating of nutmeg, then milk the cow into it until you have the amount you consider proper. Then top it off with about a half pint of sweet, thick cream."

Whipt syllabub
2 cups white wine, grated peel of 1 lemon, 1 cup sugar, 3 cups milk, 2 cups heavy cream, and 3 egg whites. Combine wine, lemon peel, and sugar. Stir to

dissolve the sugar, and add milk and cream. Beat with a rotary beater until mixture is frothy. Beat egg whites until stiff, gradually add 6 tablespoons sugar, beating constantly until the mixture forms stiff peaks. Pour wine mixture into a chilled punch bowl. Top with spoonfuls of the egg whites. Serve in chilled glasses.

Deep South Syllabub

This is another of Hortense Sager's old and rare syllabub recipes, which supposedly started "southern beaux and belles on their drunken downfall, since it was so mild that children were allowed to have it, thus acquiring a taste for the flavor of all liquors." However, she added, "of course, the idea was silly, the syllabub was delicious and the moral damage negligible." To make it for a dessert: 1 cup heavy cream, 1 egg white, 1/2 cup powdered sugar, 2 tablespoons wine or brandy, and fruits. Whip the cream with 1/4 cup of the powdered sugar until stiff. Beat the egg white with the other 1/4 cup of sugar. Combine, mixing well but lightly. Add the wine and pour over the fruits. The fruits: use 2 oranges chopped and 2 sliced bananas or 1/2 cup pineapple with the 2 oranges. Use other fruit combinations as desired.

Syllabub with Sherry

Sweeten rich milk and cream and mix. Add Sherry or Madeira to flavor and top each glassful with whipped cream.

Syllabub with Froth

1/2 pound sugar, 3 pints lukewarm cream, 1 cup wine. Dissolve sugar in the wine, then pour it on the milk from a height slowly, to cause the milk to froth, then drink.

69

from *Dining with the Cattle Barons*
by Sarah Morgan
Fort Worth
reprinted by permission of the author

Christmas at the JA

(The Goodnight ranch)

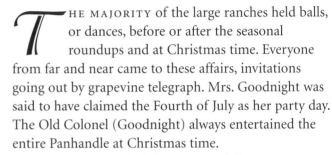

THE MAJORITY of the large ranches held balls, or dances, before or after the seasonal roundups and at Christmas time. Everyone from far and near came to these affairs, invitations going out by grapevine telegraph. Mrs. Goodnight was said to have claimed the Fourth of July as her party day. The Old Colonel (Goodnight) always entertained the entire Panhandle at Christmas time.

For weeks ahead of the appointed day women were busy planning and preparing for the big party at the Goodnight ranch, which was often attended by as many as 175 persons.

Long tables in the form of a cross were loaded with food—roast beef, wild turkey, antelope, cakes, pies, and other delicacies of the day. At the point where the long tables met was a Star Navy tomato box decorated with pieces of colored glass and pretty pebbles and covered with a spotlessly clean white cloth. Upon this central table stood the Christmas tree, a spruce or other evergreen from the Palo Duro Canyon, ornamented with bunches of frosted raisins and strings of popcorn and cranberries. Each guest received at least one present.

Dances, a favorite diversion of the time, were attended by cowboys and others from great distances. Dancing continued until the small hours of the night, or morning, rather. Girls, of whom there were never enough to go around, danced and rested alternately. Tables of food were kept ready to refresh the inner man and woman at all hours of the night. Artists of the fiddle, banjo, and guitar furnished music. "City" orchestras were imported on several occasions for special dances, such as the "protracted" dance at the White Deer ranch.

The Nussbaum brothers, owners of the White Deer range who were manufacturers of graniteware in St. Louis, sent down a carload of utensils for the occasion. There was no lack of vessels in which to cook and serve the enormous amount of food consumed at this prolonged celebration, which was held in honor of the completion of the white house or ranch headquarters. Snow and ice following subzero temperature caused the guests to remain from Christmas until New Year's Day. But a good time was had by all.

C. May Cohea
Oral History Collection
Panhandle Plains Historical Museum
Canyon

Christmas Folk Sayings

If you eat too much and get indigestion, wear
a penny around your neck.

~

If you have eaten so much your stomach is upset, turn
your medicine glass upside down under the bed.

~

Enough is as good as a feast.

~

After dinner, rest a while; after supper, walk a mile.

~

If the sun shines through an apple tree on Christmas
Day, there will be a good crop next year.

(Linck, Ernestine Sewell, and Joyce Gibson Roach.
Eats: A Folk History of Texas Foods.
Fort Worth: TCU Press, 1989: 197)

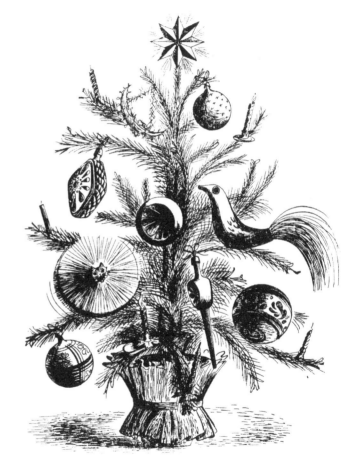

The Best Christmas

IN THE OPENING of Charles Dickens' *A Tale of Two Cities*, he wrote that it was the best of times and the worst of times. Looking back over a lifetime of pleasant Christmases, I sometimes think the best I ever had was probably in 1944. It was also the worst, for some of the same reasons that it was the best.

World War II was in its third year for the United States before I turned eighteen and received my call to service. Many of my close friends from our old high school in Crane, Texas, were a bit older and had already gone into uniform. I suffered guilt and delusions of inferiority because I was finishing my second year in college, yet was not old enough to shoulder my share of the burden. But in April 1944, President Roosevelt sent me his greetings almost before my younger brothers had eaten all of my birthday cake. I had tried to enlist in the navy at seventeen but was turned down because I had flat feet. The army willingly accepted me, however. I eventually wound up in the walking infantry, which has left me distrustful of the military mind ever since. But that is another story. I had never had a Christmas away from family. I did not look forward to Christmas of 1944.

My induction was at Fort Bliss in El Paso, then an important training ground for anti-aircraft. I was assigned to A Battery of the 56th Battalion for basic training. I found myself thrown into the company of hundreds of young men from all over the United States as well as Mexico. The army was accepting a great many young Mexican nationals. They were promised they would earn American citizenship for their service. Many did not speak English, and what some of the Yankee and deep-South sergeants could do to Spanish names bordered on the criminal. It was also hilarious. At one roll call the sergeant stumbled over several but had muddled his way through until he read, "Ga-WILL-ermo TRUDGE-illo." Nobody answered, but someone should have, for the count was right. Again, much louder and redder in the face, he shouted, "Ga-WILL-ermo TRUDGE-illo." Finally someone realized what he was trying to say and nudged Guillermo Trujillo, who shouted, "Here!" The sergeant gave him a look that said a week on KP and demanded, "Why don't you answer when you hear your name?"

I made a lot of temporary friends in that outfit, though at the time I didn't know how temporary they would be. We shared a set of five-man tarpaper shacks on the eastern edge of the post, near the air corps runways. I still remember the names, like Ralph Howery of Indiana, Hubert Langley of Arkansas, Jimmy Knapil of Ohio. We were a diverse and cosmopolitan group, a cross-section of America.

And I remember Lee Irvine, a small, quiet fellow who turned out to be the only ranch-raised boy in the outfit besides myself. He came from Buffalo, Wyoming, which sounded like a romantic Old West place to a kid from the Crane County sandhills. At the lower end of our battery area were cavalry stables that had only recently been deactivated. They still smelled of horses and hay. Nights, once in a while, I would get homesick and stray off down there to lean on the fence and sniff a little scent of home. More than once I found Lee Irvine there, doing the same thing. He was homesick too.

Our battery commander was a tough little rooster of a first lieutenant named Mergen, barrel-chested, possessed of a deep bass voice much like that of Eugene Pallette, the grand character actor of the 1930s and 1940s. With three words he could peel the hide from a recruit at a hundred yards. A top sergeant in the regular army before the war, he had a wartime commission but still was a top sergeant at heart. He was utterly without mercy, constantly driving, never pleased with anything we did, always demanding more than the human body could stand. I considered him the meanest man I had ever known, a view shared by every buck private in the outfit. Always, seemingly every time we turned around, Mergen was there, threatening, bullying, cursing.

I began to suspect that all was not as he made it seem, however. Through the Red Cross I received word that my grandfather was dying in Midland after a long struggle with a melanoma. Though army custom was that enlisted men were granted emergency leaves only for deaths in the immediate family—father, mother, siblings, wife—a sympathetic Mergen provided me a pass that got me to Midland just an hour before my grandfather died.

Christmas had always been a family time for us, and I was sure I would spend this one in a military camp scrubbing out garbage cans, not an infrequent assignment for me at Bliss. But we finished our basic training late in December, and to our pleasant surprise we were all furloughed home for the holidays. By that time the German air force, the Luftwaffe, was all but destroyed, and the army didn't need any more anti-air-craft personnel. I was ordered to report after Christmas to Camp Howze near Gainesville, Texas, for crash training in the infantry. I would be in Europe by February or March, they said, ready for front-line combat.

As we lined up to receive our individual orders, there stood the lieutenant, the monster Mergen, his eyes shining with tears. He told us something he had felt he could not tell us before: he had already been to hell and back. He knew what combat was. He had purposely made life as hard as possible for us, knowing he could never make it as hard as what some of us might be going to. He had toughened us as much as he knew how, hoping he might enable us to survive. With tears on his cheeks he asked God's blessing on us, then saluted, turned around and walked away without looking back.

It is a sad thing about wartime military life that you make friends, then lose contact with them as you are scattered in all directions. We all promised to write to one another, but most of us never did. Of all the friends with whom I stood that final afternoon on the Fort Bliss parade ground, the only one I ever saw or heard from again was Lee Irvine, the ranch boy from Wyoming. We would later sail to Europe on the same troop ship, a converted English tub so old it had a wooden hull.

The lieutenant's words, but even more the look in

his face and eyes, rode the bus home with me to what by then I feared might be my last Christmas. A dark premonition began to build, one that would not leave me until my part of the war was over. I believe every combat soldier has it, but each thinks his is the only one.

Up to that point it was a Christmas like most of my seventeen others, spent quietly on the McElroy Ranch where my father had been foreman for most of a dozen years. I hung up my uniform and put on my Levis and boots. I rode horseback and cowboyed a little, though I had never been very good at it. I had always suspected I was a disappointment to my cowboy father. My youngest brother at twelve was a better hand than I was at eighteen.

For a few days, out of uniform, I tried to put aside the dread that by now lay like a cold lump of lead in the pit of my stomach, a dread I dared not talk about to anyone, least of all my mother and father. I made up my mind that if it was to be my last Christmas, I wanted to make it my best. I gloried in the familiar faces and stored up memories that I hoped would carry me through.

In that respect it was very possibly the best Christmas I ever had, and the greatest gift was those few short days of peace and love in the only totally sane place I had ever found: home. And it was the worst, for that dread never went away. Always in an unguarded moment, in response to something someone said or a worried look I could see in someone's eyes, I would feel that chill.

It seemed a short Christmas. Almost before I realized it, I had to go to Odessa to catch the bus. There was something melancholy about bus stations in those wartime years . . . I had the same feeling about airports during the long Vietnam tragedy much later on. They were sad places, places where men too young said goodbye to wives and sweethearts and mothers and went off into a dark unknown from which they might not return.

A few years after World War II a memorial plaque I saw on a wall near the bus station in San Antonio said it all. The words as I recall were, "A few feet from this spot, a loving father said goodbye to his beloved son for the last time on this earth."

I boarded my bus with a sack of fruitcake and cookies and a stomach so cold I could not eat them. My best Christmas was over.

Camp Howze was a miserable place of hastily constructed tarpaper barracks and cold, wet winds, of coal-fired heaters and deep black mud. Gainesville was something else, however. In the downtown Methodist Church on the two or three Sundays I was able to leave the post, the people treated me with a kindness and warmth that has remained with me all these years. They gave me a prayer book that I carried with me overseas and that I still hold among my treasures. They did not take away the dread, but they gave me strength to live with it.

I made new friends at Howze, not one of whose names I can remember. The only old friend I found there was Lee Irvine. He was assigned to a different unit, but we crossed trails a few times.

After a perfunctory training session of about six or seven weeks they loaded us on troop trains, hauled us to Camp Kilmer, New Jersey, put us on troop ships and rushed us to Germany for the final stage of the European war. As always, I lost track of everyone I knew. I joined a 26th Division infantry company as a replacement the night of the Rhine River crossing. We went over in a truck convoy on a pontoon bridge the army engineers had constructed during the day under constant enemy fire.

The worst of the war was already over. Despite all my forebodings, my personal combat experience was far less dreadful than I had feared. The Germans were in full retreat. Much of the time we were ordered to ride atop Sherman tanks in the interests of speed. It was one of these tanks that took me out of the war a couple of weeks before the German surrender. It ran into a stone wall and pinned my foot, making confetti of my boot and a mess of my ankle.

I developed some idea of the enormity of the war when I watched refugees and concentration-camp survivors by the hundreds lining the roads, going somewhere, anywhere, to get away from where they had been. It was even more forcefully driven home to me on Memorial Day. I was on crutches in an army hospital outside of Paris. Those of us able to move around were offered a bus ride out to a military cemetery for services. I remember that some officers spoke, but I do not remember anything they said. What I remember was the feeling of awe and sadness as I looked at row upon row of Christian crosses and Stars of David, thousands of them stretching all the way up a gentle hillside and beyond. And flying over them, lifting and falling in a gentle wind, was the American flag. That scene has come back to me a thousand times when I look up at the stars and stripes and think of all those men—most of them young like I was—who gave all there was to give for their country.

I was a late arrival, so I was obliged to stay for a little more than a year after the war in Europe had ended. I spent the Christmas of 1945 in Austria, with the family of a young woman who was to become my wife and whose lingering accent and phonetic spelling were to provide amusement to our children and grandchildren for years to come. It was a long way from home, and the holiday customs were in many ways different from those I had known, but it has always remained a stand-out Christmas for me, as 1944 has always been.

In the first years after coming home I sent Christmas cards to some of my old army friends, or tried to. Most of the cards came back undelivered. Often I would wonder about this one or that one and what had ever become of him. Among others, I wondered about the boy from Wyoming.

In my later career as a livestock journalist, I sometimes found myself in the company of stockmen from other parts of the country. Several times I met ranch people from Wyoming. I would always ask if they had ever heard of Lee Irvine. Always I drew a blank.

It was thirty years after the war when one day at the office of the *Livestock Weekly* I received a letter from Van Irvine of Casper, Wyoming, inquiring about advertising rates. He wanted to auction off a big band of sheep. I answered his query and at the end of the letter casually asked him if he might be kin to my Wyoming friend of Fort Bliss days.

A few days later I received his reply. Lee Irvine had been his kid brother, he said. He was killed in April 1945, a few days after arrival in Germany.

Thirty years fell away in an instant, and the feeling of grief was as strong as if the loss had just happened. I just sat there awhile, frozen.

I have had sixty Christmases since 1944. But it was the last for Lee Irvine and for others I knew. It was the last Christmas in which the world seemed young.

It was in some ways the best Christmas I ever had. It was also my worst.

Elmer Kelton
San Angelo

Some Christmas Memories

I Was Grown Before I Ever Knew You Was Supposed to Have a Christmas Tree
BILL CLEVELAND

At school we'd have a Christmas tree. We didn't have much on it. The teachers would usually buy you something—a handkerchief or something like that was as much as you ever got. Usually the school would have apples and oranges for ever'body. We decorated the tree with popcorn and paper links, paper chains. Some of the men would cut the tree out of the cedar breaks. We didn't have a tree at home. I was grown before I ever knew you was supposed to have a Christmas tree. Us kids would take a branch off of the tree at school and take it home. And that was as near as I ever knew of having a Christmas tree.

People Had Christmas Then, and It Didn't Cost No Big Bucks
CLYDE HODGES

We usually got out of school some for holidays. For Christmas they'd dismiss 'bout three or four days. We didn't even know there was any Thanksgiving going on, and we didn't know then what Halloween was.

Sometimes people'd pull tricks on each other at Christmas. I remember when Christmastime come, they would pull tricks on the neighbors. Dad had a surrey. Me and the kids thought more of that surrey than we did the first automobile we ever got. We got up one morning, and it was sitting up on top of the roof of the house. Some one had come in the night and put it on the roof of the house. Yeah, seven or eight big stout men, you know, they set that surrey up on the roof of the house. They come back and helped get it down. Same ones that put it up. That was at Christmastime, just for fun.

Oh, I tell you what. People had Christmas then, and it didn't cost no big bucks. You could take Christmas night then, and you could look all over the country, and the sky would be full of skyrockets 'til midnight. Some of them all night long. You could buy a whole bunch of Christmas fireworks. Didn't cost much.

For Christmas we'd get a pair of socks, an apple, or an orange. Ever' kid then hung up a sock on the fireplace. It'd be filled with fruit, candy, and apples, and maybe the sock wouldn't hold it all, so there'd be some sitting down on each side of the fireplace. I tell you what, kids then got a lot of Christmas presents that they thought a lot of. Each of the cousins back then would buy or make a Christmas present for the other cousins, you know. And you could get a pair of good socks then for twenty-five cents.

(*The Empty School House: Memories of One-Room Texas Schools,* compiled and edited by Luther Bryan Clegg. College Station: Texas A&M Press, 1997: 119-120)

In Search of Uncle Freddie

Almost anyone can tell you the year when the Great Depression began—1929. That's when the government, who was a great noticer of things after they happened, said it began. The date the Depression ended was more personal depending upon who you were and where you were at the time. My name was Joyce Ann Gibson, and I lived in a small town on the edge of the plains. Who I was, where I was, and growing up where I did marked me for life in a certain way, and consequently that period of time shaped me for all seasons to come. Some memories you never get away from, nor am I trying. The end of the Depression is marked in my memory's calendar as December 7, 1941—Pearl Harbor Day.

Thanksgiving of 1941 was wonderful. While it sounds undemocratic, unpatriotic, and unrealistic to admit it, I loved the Depression. Nobody had anything, but we all had plenty of nothing together in the same proportions and at the same time so that no one felt inferior or left out. We all shared material inferiority together, and we wore it like a badge. There was enough food on my table.

My daddy had a job. My mother specialized in Good Mothership; Uncle Freddie and Mama Hartman were with us. It had always been so since time began for me, and it would always be so. Amen and Amen.

We had a fine Thanksgiving dinner. There were family stories from Mama Hartman. She was the only teller and I the only listener, but what she had to say then assured me later that I was truly kin to the family of man. Later my daddy and my Uncle Freddie took me hunting. We didn't shoot anything that day. We never did for that matter. Somehow we were always too early or too late for the deer or the turkey, or the quail. One time we did fire a gun though when we went out to Audy Weir's place to hunt. We couldn't scare up a thing. Ice covered the ground (no snow), and we slipped and slid toward home in our Ford. Suddenly Uncle Fred slammed on the brakes and hollered, "Ducks, ducks on the pond." We all jumped out and started running. "Don't run, don't run. You'll scare the ducks. Crawl. We got to get down on our hands and knees and crawl." There was certainly some good, sound logic to that advice. Down we went, our stomachs and elbows against the ice and cold. Slowly, ever so slowly, up and over the dam of the tank and down to the water's edge

we crawled. Our legs and feet were now much higher than our heads. Then like Custer at the Big Horn my uncle bellowed, "Shoot, Dave, shoot!" Daddy came up like gang busters, aimed his gun, fired and fell full face into the icy tank. Feathers flew but no duck was harmed. We went home wet and cold and happy in the knowledge that the story would become a classic in the chapters of the family saga.

Christmas of 1941 would find us thinking again about guns. No missed ducks or turkey or deer would fall under the weapons, but instead flesh and blood, perhaps the flesh and blood of the men in my own family. On December 7, 1941, I was visiting Uncle Lyndon in Eastland, Texas. We were getting ready to go home when President Roosevelt's voice came over the radio telling about a place called Pearl Harbor and a day of infamy. We were at war and before I would see my beloved Freddie again, three Christmases would come and go.

The war was terribly exciting. It was almost as good as the Depression. Again the citizens of Jacksboro pulled together, and the war kept us bound together. There were parades. I dressed up as a nurse and put red and blue crepe paper in the spokes of my bicycle. I learned how to play, "In my arms, in my arms," on the violin. We all collected tin foil and made it into great round balls. I can feel the weight of it yet in my hands. It pleased me wonderfully to think that bullets and bombs would grow from that metal and kill many of the enemy. Oh, don't think I didn't know who the enemy was. Every night I got down on my knees with my grandmother and prayed that God would stop those "boot stomping Germans and those runty Japs." God knew what was what and who was who and he was on our side, or at least he was on my grandmother's side.

My daddy in those days was a butcher for Safeway stores. As it turned out he was the only man left in all Jack Country who had a permit from the government to butcher and distribute beef. Almost every Sunday after church, where we prayed that God would smite the heathen, Daddy, Mother and I would go to the county, select a cow, shoot him or knock him in the head, string him up over a tree limb and butcher the daylights out of him. I liked to see how easily the hide slid off an old, dead cow and how neatly all the entrails came spilling out in a pile. The rest was just a matter of hacking and sawing and it was all done. I enjoyed every minute of it. To add a little to our Christmas money my daddy saved all the hides, bones, and fat from those Sunday expedi-

tions. When he had a good trailer full, the family headed to Ft. Worth to the soap factory. We were noticeable both by sight and smell. Once while pulling a long hill near Springtown, the trailer came loose. As it rolled back down, hides, bones, and fat flew all over the road. Cars swerved, Mother screamed. After Daddy got the car stopped, he ran down the hill acting as if somehow he could stop that trailer. By the time we got to him, he was

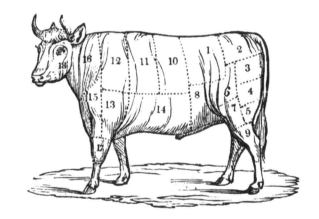

standing in the middle of the road, assorted colored hides and cow bones clasped to his bosom. When the constabulary arrived to survey the damage spread over half-mile of highway and to reroute the traffic, Daddy said, "If you'll just give me a minute I'll think of what to do about this mess." They tell me the smell lingered for days, and Daddy never did think of what to do.

I couldn't put my finger on just when the war changed from a child's game to a horrid maw that threatened to swallow us all. Sugar rationing and no tires and no hose weren't really all that bad. It was rather a feeling, an atmosphere that settled over the town and especially over my home. My daddy's bag stayed always packed and sitting near the door. They were taking the younger boys first but some of the fathers of my friends were gone already. A large group of Jacksboro men were among the famous Lost Battalion, and somewhere in the steaming jungles they were indeed lost to us, starved and pitiful and maybe worse off than dead. We saw war newsreels at the movies, and then the telegrams begin to arrive. Sons and husbands and fathers were only stars that hung in the windows, the number of men serving designated by the number of stars in the window.

There were two stars on the window of my own home. My Uncle Glen was in Africa with the army chasing Rommel the Desert Fox. Finally Glen returned to us

WWII Star—Collection of Barbara M.Whitehead

wounded and torn from a shell that hit his tank and killed all but him.

My beloved Uncle Freddie with his laughter and rough ways was in the navy. I felt somehow that he was safer on a big ship. I did not know until much later that he manned a smaller boat that took the troops ashore on Iwo Jima. His ship was the S.S. *Blackhawk*. Mama Hartman and Mother and I prayed for Glen and Fred and so strong were my grandmother's prayers that although they might be wounded I knew that the Great God of the Righteous would surely not let them die.

It was with all these burdens resting on us that I looked toward the third Christmas of the war. Wonder of wonder, my Uncle Freddie was coming home. He didn't call us until he got stateside so that we wouldn't be disappointed if he didn't make it for Christmas day. There was a tree with all the trimmings and a turkey in the oven, but there was no ice that Christmas. In fact it was so warm that I played all day in a cotton dress and barefooted. I worried and stewed and thought of all I would say. I threw the ball for Scottie, my dog, until late afternoon and still no Uncle Fred. I finally saw a man in a navy uniform turn the corner and begin walking down the dusty, unpaved street. It wasn't my Uncle Freddie. He had dark hair. This man had white hair. But something about the way he walked and held his shoulders told me that it was my uncle. I hollered at Mother and then flew down the street only to stop short, square in the strange man's path. He bent down and asked sadly in a voice not his own if I wanted a piggyback ride. I grabbed hold and laid my cheek on his now snow white head and cried and cried and suddenly came of age.

I knew without being told that war was truly horrible if it could take away my uncle's dark hair. He had participated in dark and bloody deeds so terrible that he never spoke of them until forty years later. Fred seemed barely human, but it was the happiest, saddest, best, worst Christmas I ever spent in my life. We thought there was nothing we could do for Fred, but I know that one human being was stirred and restored to life that very Christmas by the tears of his niece, his sister, and his mother.

It was a good Depression. It was good War. And it's good that both are in the past.

Joyce Gibson Roach
Keller

85

The Boar's Head Festival

Each year, members of the congregation of University Christian Church in Fort Worth turn into angels, Renaissance ladies and gentlemen, wise men and shepherds, English Beefeater Guards, dancing sprites and wood elves, joining together to present an extravagant version of the traditional Renaissance Boar's Head Festival. The hour-long festival fills the church with joyful music of choir, orchestra, pealing church bells, and a carefully modulated bell choir. In many spots, the congregation is invited to join the singing of familiar carols such as "Good King Wenceslas" and "Angles We Have Heard on High." It is a true celebration involving young and old, participants and congregation.

According to the ancient legend behind this festival, an Oxford University student was strolling in a forest, reading the works of Aristotle, when a wild and raging boar charged him. Thinking quickly, the student thrust the volume of Aristotle down the boar's throat; the animal choked and fell dead. Later, the slaughtered boar's head was carried back to Oxford for a feast, and the celebration of the saving of the student's life came to represent the triumph of reason over brute force.

The Church adapted the festival and gave it Christian significance, with the boar's head, a symbolic representation of evil, overcome by good through the teachings of Christ, symbolized by light. It became a part of the celebration of Epiphany, which marks the visit of three wise men to the infant Jesus. Dating back at least to the fourteenth century, this is the oldest continuing festival of the Christmas season and was a holiday tradition in many great manor houses in England before it was brought to America in colonial days.

The festival opens with the heavy tread of the Beefeaters, traditional guardians of the English King, as they take their places in the narthex and aisles to stand their Watch of Honor. Then, slowly moving through the silent darkness, a tiny sprite, always played by a child from a church family, carries a single taper to the altar and, with the minister, lights the Christ Candle and holds it high so that its blessed light may shine on all gathered.

To the tune of the "Boar's Head Carol," the story unfolds as the boar's head is brought into the sanctuary and carried to the altar by companies of knights who are preceded by a black banner, symbolizing darkness, and banners for Christ who overcomes it. The head is followed by plum puddings, fruitcakes, a giant mince pie, and other goods suggesting the fullness of God's gifts to his children. In motley, loving company, the greatest and the humblest follow the board to Christ's altar—kings and noblemen, huntsmen and cooks, pilgrim and pauper, and troops of God's favorites, the children.

The festival continues with the bringing in of the Yule Log, the story of King Wenceslas, and the dancing and hijinx of the waits, poor boys who wait on tables. Then, beginning with a musical rendition of the angel's announcement to the shepherds, the festival builds to the climactic moment when the triptych is opened to reveal Mary, Joseph, and the Baby. All the participants in the festival have by then returned to the altar area to bring their gifts to the Christ Child and to kneel in adoration. The moment when the Beefeater guards open the triptych, symbolizing God's gift of love and light to mankind through Christ, can only be described as breathtaking.

The triptych is closed, and the assembled company drifts away, leaving behind the Christ Candle. The Yule Sprite returns and together, the minister and the sprite—experience and innocence—joyfully carry the candle from the church, taking God's love into the world. The Reverend A. M. Pennybacker, who was senior minister of the church twenty-eight years ago when the first festival was held, established the tradition of skipping. To this day, the minister and the sprite skip the length of the church as they leave.

And, for many in the congregation, the Boar's Head Festival, performed on Saturday and Sunday the weekend after New Year's Day, brings the Christmas season to an end and marks the time to go back to the real world. Like the joyful carrying forth of the candle, the festival ends the season with a sense of joy.

Judy Alter
Fort Worth

A Carol of the Gift of God

How can it be? the force that gave
Both time and space their powers—
How can it stoop to bind itself,
Inhabit flesh like ours?
Alleluia, sing alleluia, sing all alleluia.
We who are dust motes in the sun
That He should magnify
Us with his love, such shining truth
I cannot reason why.
To see if it be safe for us,
A King should taste of death!
Test the thin garment of our days
By putting on our breath!
Come brothers, sisters, sing.
Sing for joy! Sing alleluia!
The gift of God make known
Is wrapped in tissue and in trim
As mortal as our own!
Alleluia, sing alleluia, sing all alleluia.

William D. Barney   *Fort Worth*
    1983 Poet Laureate of Texas

89

Postcard—Collection of Darnelle Vanghel

Contributors

JUDY ALTER is the author of fiction for adults and young adults and has won honors from Western Writers of America, the Texas Institute of Letters, the Children's Book Council, and the Voice of Youth Advocates. Her most recent book is *Sam Houston Is My Hero*. Alter serves as director of TCU Press.

The late WILLIAM BARNEY, a Fort Worth postal inspector, was named poet laureate of Texas in the 1980s and received the Robert Frost Award for Poetry in New York City from Frost himself. Two of his books, *Kneel for the Stone* and *Permitted Proof,* received awards from the Texas Institute of Letters.

The late C. MAY COHEA contributed her memories of Christmas at the JA Ranch as an oral history interview to the Panhandle Plains Museum in Canyon.

The late MINETTA ALTGELT GOYNE grew up in the German communities of Central Texas and taught English and German literature at the University of Texas, TCU, Louisiana State University, Texas Wesleyan University, and the University of Texas at Arlington.

HELEN GREEN was the first black woman admitted to a school of professional nursing in Dallas in the 1960s. She has written a memoir, *East Texas Daughter,* about her childhood, her struggle for education, and her career in nursing and nursing administration. She makes her home in DeSoto.

ELMER KELTON of San Angelo is the author of over forty novels dealing with Texas history from the days of the Republic to the present. He has won numerous awards from the National Cowboy Hall of Fame, Western Writers of America, and other organizations. His most recent book is *The Way of the Coyote.*

JAS. MARDIS has published three volumes of poetry— *Southern Tongue, Hanging Times,* and *The Ticking and The Time Going Past*—and edited the anthology, *Kente Cloth: Southwestern Voices of the African Diaspora.* His "Invisible Man," published in *Kente Cloth,* received the 2000 Pushcart Prize.

PAT MORA, an award-winning author of children's books, poetry, and nonfiction, is devoted to creative writing, leadership, and multicultural education. *A Library for Juana: the World of Sor Juana Inéz* (English and Spanish editions) received the 2003 Tomás Rivera Mexican American Children's Book Award, and *María Paints the Hills* was a finalist for the Texas Institute of Letters Best Children's Book, 2003.

The late SARAH MORGAN was a restaurateur, cookbook author, authority on Texas food, and long a beloved member of the TCU community.

PAUL PATTERSON is a retired teacher and writer from Sierra Blanca and Crane who writes about folks and events in far West Texas. He is a longtime member of the Texas Folklore Society and still attends its meetings, in spite of his ninety-plus years.

The late FREDA POWELL taught drama at Sul Ross University in Alpine and was founding director of the Carillion Theater on the South Campus of Fort Worth's Tarrant County College.

About the Editor

FIFTH-generation Texan JOYCE GIBSON ROACH is an award-winning author and folklorist. Her books include *The Cowgirls, Eats: A Folk History of Texas Foods, This Place of Memory, Collective Heart, Wild Rose,* and the children's books, *Horned Toad Canyon* and *Cowgirl of the Rocking R.* She makes her home in Keller and on a family ranch in Wise County.

TEXAS *and* CHRISTMAS

Set in Minion with Isadora display

Design and Production by BARBARA M. WHITEHEAD, Austin

2004

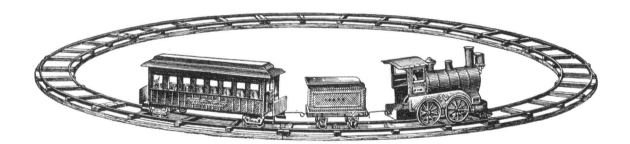